RED GUIDE

The Lake District

Including
Walking and Motoring Routes

Edited by Reginald J. W. Hammond

Thirty-second edition

WARD LOCK LIMITED
116 Baker Street, London, W.1
and at Sydney

Maps

Contents

CONTENTS

THE CENTRAL DISTRICT

The Southern, or Windermere, Section

CONTENTS

The Northern, or Keswick, Section

The Eastern, or Ullswater, Section

The Western Section

The Passes

THE OUTER DISTRICT

The Coastal Section

The Inland Section

Illustrations

 — ISBN 0 7063 5438 9

Printed in Great Britain by
Cox and Wyman Limited, London, Fakenham and Reading

Introducing the Lake District

The "Lake District" proper has been defined as the "picturesque and mountainous region comprised within the counties of Westmorland and Cumberland and a small portion of Lancashire, within which are grouped as many as seventeen lakes or meres, besides innumerable mountain tarns and streams, and a series of mountains rising in seven points to a height of over three thousand feet. The district extends about thirty miles from north to south, by about twenty-five from east to west"; but for the benefit of visitors to this most inviting land our work covers a wider area, and some of the beautiful and interesting places beyond the defined boundary are dealt with.

For the sake of clarity and convenience the area covered by the Guide is divided into two main districts, with sections as listed below. A glance at the Contents pages will make the arrangement of the book clear.

I. THE CENTRAL DISTRICT

1. The Southern or Windermere Section.
2. The Northern or Keswick Section.
3. The Eastern or Ullswater Section.
4. The Western Section.
5. The Passes.

II. THE OUTER DISTRICT

1. The Coastal Section.
2. The Inland Section.

Gray, the poet, is generally credited with having "discovered" the Lake District, which he visited in 1769, and his journal, *A Tour in the Lakes*, was certainly the first book in which an attempt was successfully made to present a faithful idea of the rich and varied beauties of the country.

Within a few years of Gray's visit the first *Guide to the*

Lakes was published by Father West who made the following claims in his introduction:

> "Such as wish to unbend the mind from anxious cares or fatiguing studies, will meet with agreeable relaxation in making the tour of the lakes. Something new will open itself at the turn of every mountain, and a succession of ideas will be supported by a perpetual change of objects, and a display of scenes behind scenes in endless perspective. . . . Such as spend their lives in cities, and their time in crowds, will here meet with objects that will enlarge the mind, by contemplation, and raise it from nature to nature's first cause."

It was, however, neither guide-books, nor industrial progress that "opened up" the Lake District, but Wordsworth, Southey, the Coleridges (father and son), Wilson ("Christopher North"), De Quincey, and, afterwards, Mrs. Hemans, Harriet Martineau, Arnold of Rugby, and John Ruskin. The gifted Dorothy Wordsworth, though last-named, was in many ways one of the most charming of all that brilliant intellectual galaxy. But the greatest of all was William Wordsworth. Almost all that has since been penned about Lakeland has found its note of inspiration in his poems.

Routes to the Lakes

Railway Routes

The Lake District is encircled by lines of the London Midland Region of British Rail. From Lancaster, running north for 70 miles along the east boundary of the Lake District, the main Euston—Carlisle rail route provides services to Oxenholme with its branch line through Kendal into the centre of Southern Lakeland at Windermere.

Continuing northwards the route serves Penrith giving access to Ullswater Lake, before reaching Carlisle. For the tourist wishing to get into the heart of the Northern Lakes, the Penrith—Keswick line penetrates westwards into the area, bringing the scenic beauty around Lakes Derwentwater and Bassenthwaite within easy reach.

Taking the coastal rail route, again starting at Lancaster, this winds westwards to Arnside, Grange-over-Sands and Ulverston to Barrow-in-Furness, all of which are good centres for short road journeys into the Lake District. After Barrow the route turns to the north for Foxfield, continuing by Duddon estuary to Millom, passes Silecroft for Black Combe, and on to Ravenglass from where runs the famous narrow-gauge railway up Eskdale to Dalegarth Station, near the foot of Scafell. The next station of interest is Seascale for the Wasdale district, then comes Whitehaven and finally Workington, the line continuing from there to join the main line again at Carlisle.

Road Routes to the District

In the following summary of main roads of approach to the Lake Country Keswick is the centre chosen, because from all sides it is easily reached over easy passes and by good roads.

The roads from Liverpool (*via* Ormskirk, 31 m.), Manchester (*via* Bolton and Horwich, 31 m.), and Warrington (*via* Ashton-in-Makerfield and Wigan, 29½ m.), converge on **Preston.** The scenery in South Lancashire is tame, and the roads are marred by industrial traffic, though the Preston and Lancaster motorway (M6) now provides an excellent very fast run. After Lancaster, across Morecambe Bay, the distant fells are visible. From Carnforth (27¾ m.) through Milnthorpe (35 m.), the road passes Levens Hall, and at Kendal (42¾ m.) reaches the edge of the real Lake Country. The route (A591) to Keswick (72 m.) is through Windermere and Ambleside (55½ m.).

From London and Southern England the best route is *via* the Great North Road to within 2 miles of Wetherby (200 m. from London), thence *via* Collingham, Harewood, Ilkley, Skipton, Settle and Kirkby Lonsdale to Kendal (269 m. from London). There are, however, numerous alternatives, which though not so fast running, provide better scenery and less traffic.

From the south-east, the best road may be taken as starting from Leeds, and passing through Otley and Ilkley to Skipton (25 m.). From Settle (42½ m.) to Kirkby Lonsdale (60 m.), the road (A65) is hilly. At Kendal (72¾ m.) the road for Windermere (81 m.) and Keswick (102 m.) is joined.

Another and longer route from Leeds to Keswick goes at first northward to Harrogate (15 m.) and Ripon (26½ m.), thence working westward *via* Middleham (44¾ m.), Leyburn (47 m.), and beautiful Wensleydale to Hawes (63½ m.). From this village to the *Moorcock Inn* (69 m.) is mostly rise, and at the inn the road forks, a direct route west falling down Garsdale to Sedbergh and Kendal (89½ m.), whence the Windermere (98 m.) road is followed to Keswick (119 m.). The steep hill 2 miles east of Kendal is generally avoided by a left turn near the seventh milestone from Sedbergh, but at the top of the hill on the direct road a glorious view of the town and distant fells is sighted. The north fork at the *Moorcock* (69 m.) leads to Kirkby Stephen (80½ m.), Brough (84½ m.) and traverses the lovely Eden Valley to Penrith (105 m.), thence west by Troutbeck and Threlkeld to Keswick (123 m.).

From Newcastle and the north-east the most direct route is by Alston (45 m.) to Penrith (64¾ m.) and Keswick (82¾ m.), but the road is very hilly, and between Alston and Penrith Hartside pass rises 1,889 feet above the sea. There is an alternative route (A69) *via* Hexham (21½ m.), Haltwhistle

(37 m.), Brampton (50 m.), Carlisle (59 m.), and Keswick (9¼ m.). There is a direct route from Carlisle *via* Bothel to Keswick (91½ m.), the latter part of the road passing close to the shores of Bassenthwaite Lake.

From Scotland Carlisle (32½ m. from Keswick) is the converging point. From Glasgow there is a pleasant "Burns Country" run *via* Kilmarnock (22 m.), Mauchline (31 m.), Cummock (38 m.), Sanquhar (45 m.), Dumfries (81 m.) to Gretna (104½ m.), Carlisle (115 m.) and Keswick (147½ m.).

There is a shorter Clyde route over Beattock: Hamilton (12½ m.), Abington (37½ m.), Beattock (57½ m.), Lockerbie (70½ m.), Carlisle (95 m.). From Edinburgh there are also alternative routes south, the shorter is *via* Liberton (3¼ m.), Leadburn (13 m.), Romanno Bridge (19¾ m.), Crook Inn (35½ m.), Moffat (52 m.), to Carlisle (91½ m.) and Keswick (124 m.).

Another route traverses the Scott Country, through Dalkeith (6 m.), Galashiels (32 m.), Melrose (36 m.), Abbotsford (40 m.), Selkirk (44 m.), Hawick (56 m.), Langholm (79 m.), to Carlisle (100 m.). On these routes the best scenery from Glasgow lies between Sanquhar and Thornhill. The road from Edinburgh by Crook Inn gives glorious moorland views, but is somewhat severe. The reverse of the Beeftubs Pass from Moffat is rather a big task. The Scott route is easier, more picturesque, and not much the longer.

There are innumerable variations and side-routes more or less recommendable, but the roads named have been chosen from personal acquaintance.

For Motoring in the District, *see* p. 46.

Accommodation

Hotels — Youth Hostels — Camping and Caravanning.

Hotels, etc.

In all the principal touring centres excellent hotels and boarding houses are to be found, and in many of the outlying villages there are good inns. Many establishments are mentioned throughout this guide under the appropriate headings in the descriptive pages that follow. Almost everywhere there are cottages and farm houses ready to satisfy the most exacting requirements, particularly good appetites.

Whenever possible, accommodation should be secured well in advance, particularly in July, August and the early part of September. Indeed, those dependent on such facilities would be ill-advised to tour the district without having made advance reservations. Lists of establishments are always available from the local councils of the various centres.

Youth Hostels

The Youth Hostels Association have many hostels throughout the district. Hostel-users must be equipped with a sheet sleeping-bag but there is no need to carry blankets. Meals are generally provided. Full information on membership and location of the many hostels is available on application to the National Office, Trevelyan House, 8 St. Stephen's Hill, St. Albans, Herts. Tel: St. Albans 55215.

Camping

To the camper the Lake District has much to offer. Camp sites vary from the well-appointed commercial sites near popular tourist centres to the more remote farm sites so attractive to the experienced camper.

Some will prefer to use a recognised site as a base from which to explore, but undoubtedly the best way to see the district is to tour, carrying the camp kit. A good lightweight tent is essential and the addition of a flysheet very desirable. The camper who makes the right approach will rarely be refused permission to pitch his tent for the night.

The Camping Club of Great Britain (11 Lower Grosvenor Place, London, S.W.1.) gives details of some 50 Lake District sites in the list of sites issued to its members. The Club, which specialises in mobile lightweight camping, urges all campers to maintain the highest possible standards and to play their part in preserving the natural beauty of the countryside.

Caravanning

One of the pleasantest and most thorough ways of seeing the Lake District is by caravan. The Lake District Planning Board have consulted the Caravan Club about the needs of caravanners in the Park area, and their policy caters for these needs. Individual touring caravanners are not discouraged but their caravans should be pitched discreetly to avoid spoiling other people's views of the countryside. Commercial sites are allowed only where they are well screened—not, for example, at a dale head. Details of caravan sites in the district are given in the club Sites Directory (free to members). Members of the Club are exempt from certain restrictions under health and planning legislation. In particular members are allowed to make more frequent use of unlicensed sites and have substantial freedom from planning control. Club Offices are at 65, South Molton Street, London, W.1.

Travel in Lakeland

By Rail

British Rail enables the tourist to reach the hearts of both North and South Lakeland, at Windermere and Keswick. From almost any town served by the encircling rail routes, there are convenient road services to all the areas not served by rail.

Bus and Coach Services

The Lake District is so compact and the motor-coach service so good that a run of an hour or two from any of the large centres will take one to almost any part of the District that is accessible by road. The one set of road excursions is therefore common to all the tourist resorts, the most convenient centres being Windermere, Ambleside and Keswick.

The touring arrangements in the district are excellent. There is also a large number of public bus services between the principal centres, but it should be noted that there are only occasional buses to the more remote valleys, such as the Duddon and Buttermere. Throughout the district there are numerous garages where cars may be hired for long or short periods.

Details of the numerous motor-coach services linking the Lake District with most of the large towns in Britain are too variable to be quoted here, and readers are therefore referred to current announcements.

Steamers and Motor-Boats

A regular service of motor vessels runs on Windermere during the summer months, between Lake Side, Bowness and Waterhead; and on Ullswater from Pooley Bridge to Howtown and Glenridding. There is also a service of motor-boats round Derwentwater, calling at Barrow, Lodore and two stops at Brandelhow: and motor-boat trips are frequently arranged on Windermere from the three principal "ports."

Cycling

Cycling in Lakeland is enjoyable, if arduous, and is made more than usually worth while by the fact that the cyclist can often go where the motorist cannot. Cyclists should note that some of the by-roads are still crossed by gates, which are generally closed. It is important to remember that many of the valleys are "dead-ends" and tracks marked on maps may appear to be possible but often are only suitable for walkers.

Cycling in the outlying districts is less severe. The ups and downs, however, are numerous though the views obtained are well worth the hard hill climbs. Cyclists should note that there is no road for them where the railway crosses the mouths of the Kent, Leven, Duddon and Esk, and that in the case of the first two of these rivers a considerable detour inland is necessary.

Cyclists should also note that on the following passes the surfaces are good but the gradients steep: Kirkstone, Buttermere Hause, Whinlatter, Dunmail Raise, Honister. Hardknott, Wrynose, Garburn, are scarcely negotiable. The rest are *emphatically* unrideable. (*See also* p. 123.)

For Roads of the Lake District, *see* p. 46.

Climate and Seasons

There is a popular delusion that because the Lake District contains the wettest inhabited spot in England it always rains there. Many jests have been made on the subject including one—

"Not one day
In a Lake-week deserves the name of *Sun*day."

Mountain districts are naturally wet, and when it rains in Lakeland it very often *does* rain enough in an hour to satisfy a London rain-gauge for a day. One remark we have often heard—that the weather cannot spoil the Lakeland scenery. This is very true but hardly applies when the view is blotted out by rain or mist. To appreciate the beauties of the district, however, one must see them in haze, cloud, and even storm, as well as in the glory of sunshine.

One reason indeed why the tourist is seldom stormbound in Lakeland is that the dwellings, even in the remotest daleheads, are rarely six hundred feet above sea-level, and that mountain conditions such as ruin holidays in more elevated districts simply do not often occur.

The climate in the valleys is mild but not unhealthy. We have said that when it rains it *does* rain; to this may be added that when it blows it *does* blow. A fellside gale is a thing to be respected, and people who have not experienced its violence can have little conception of the force and fury of the wind.

At what season should one visit the Lakes? Our reply is at *any* time; they are always beautiful. Fine weather, of course, cannot be guaranteed, but of the spring and summer months we have generally found the end of May, early June and September with the lowest rainfall. Spring in Lakeland is lovely, but lovely too is the season of the changing leaf.

Lakeland Sports

Angling — Boating — Bowls — Golf — Mountaineering — Sailing — Tennis — Winter Sports.

Angling

Salmon are found in the rivers Leven, Duddon, Esk, Irt, Calder, Ehen, Derwent, Cocker and Eden, Eamont and Lowther (and occasionally in certain lakes); char in Windermere, Coniston Water, Goats Water, Haweswater, Derwentwater, Buttermere, Crummock Water, Ennerdale and Wastwater; brown trout nearly everywhere in lakes, rivers, becks, and tarns, while there are sea trout in the Kent, Leven, Crake, Duddon, Esk, Irt, Calder, Ehen, Derwent and Cocker. The fishing in Ullswater is free but a Cumberland River Authority licence is necessary. On the Eamont, running out of Ullswater, a mile below the lake, begin the four miles belonging to the Penrith Angling Association. Below Eamont Bridge (salmon) the water belongs to the Yorkshire Angling Association.

The coarse fish are of little account, the roach being mostly confined to the river Kent and the Kendal and Preston Canal; the tench, to muddy ponds; the chub, to the Eden streams; and the skelly, or gwyniad, to parts of Ullswater and Haweswater; whilst pike and perch are to be found almost everywhere. Perhaps the best pike fishing is to be had in Esthwaite Water, and Bassenthwaite is famous for its perch (locally "bass"). Grayling are to be found in upper reaches of the Eden.

Anglers are reminded that according to the River Boards Act it is essential to obtain, where provision is made, a current rod licence before commencing to fish in any water within a River Authority's area.

There are, of course, very many stretches of private water

which are not open to the public—*e.g.* at Isel on the Derwent, along the river Lowther, and at Levens on the Kent—but with these and a few other exceptions, a good deal of water is available. It is always as well for anglers to make enquiries before fishing.

The addresses of the respective River Authorities who issue the requisite licences and from whom much information is obtainable are as follows:

Cumberland River Authority, 256 London Road, Carlisle.

Lancashire River Authority, 48 West Cliff, Preston.

Bathing

It is hardly necessary to state that the various lakes and rivers offer abundant opportunities for bathing, and there is little restriction anywhere. On Windermere there are organised bathing places at Millerground and Waterhead; on Derwentwater there is one at the Isthmus; but to many bathing in the Lake District means a dip in an ice-cold, rock-bound pool in a mountain stream.

Bathing in the lakes and tarns is dangerous for non-swimmers owing to the steeply-shelving shores which are a trap for the unwary.

Boating

is to be had on Windermere, Derwentwater, Bassenthwaite, Crummock Water, Loweswater, Ullswater, Coniston Water, Buttermere, Esthwaite and Grasmere. Visitors are specially warned that the lakes are liable to sudden squalls of great violence from the mountains and that constant vigilance is essential to safety.

Bowls

At the larger centres such as Keswick, Ambleside and Windermere, one or more good bowling greens will generally be found on which visitors may play.

Golf

Golfing facilities are rather more on the outskirts than actually within the district. The best links are at *Seascale* and *Penrith*. There are 18-hole courses at Grange-over-Sands (also a 9-hole), Kendal, Penrith, Seascale, Ulverston, Walney Island (Barrow), Cockermouth and Windermere. And there are 9-hole courses situated at St. Bees, Sedbergh, Silecroft and Silverdale.

Mountain Walking

This form of recreation can only be enjoyed to the full by the stronger walkers and to these the country presents infinite attractions and some perils. There is not much danger if two or more companions wander over the mountains in ordinary weather; but a solitary tourist may get nervous and bewildered —especially if caught in a mist, or benighted—and is many hours (even days) wandering about, or, worse still, be incapacitated by a sprained ankle or other injury, and perhaps will finally succumb, though all the time within reach of help and safety.

New-comers to the district should not assume that in all cases where a route is referred to in the Guide, or even where a path is marked on the map, there is a definite and identifiable track for the whole distance. On some much-frequented routes (*e.g.* the path over Scarf Gap) there is a well-marked track for the whole way, and a further safeguard is provided by the cairns placed at short intervals. On other routes a definite track may exist for only a part of the way, and cairns, if they exist at all, are a long way apart. In many places it is necessary to plan a route convenient to oneself, having regard to gradients, swamps, streams, etc., and if one plans a good route one will frequently find nail scratches or other evidence that it has been trodden by previous users.

It must be remembered that for all but nursery expeditions there are five requisites. Properly nailed boots, map, compass, plenty to eat and *good condition.*

NOTE.—*Compass-bearings must be taken at the first sign of mist, not after the mist has formed.*

Rock Climbing

It must be borne in mind that the standard in the Lake District is even dangerously high, and that the recognised climbs are *not* for ordinary tourists.

Some of the notable "climbing grounds" may be viewed from the ordinary tourist tracks. Pavey Ark towers above Stickle Tarn (p. 82). Farther up Langdale, between Harrison Stickle and Pike o' Stickle, is the sheer bastion of Gimmer Crag. Dow Crags are well seen from the Old Man (p. 84) and even better from Goats (Gaits) Water. The Scafell Crags are conspicuous on the right during the latter part of the ascent of Scafell Pike from Wasdale, and Pike Crag directly overlooks the ascent. Great End faces Sprinkling Tarn and Kern Knotts are close to the Sty Head (p. 127), from which point during the descent to Wasdale the Napes Ridges stand out high upon the right. Gable Crag presents a noble front both towards Scarf Gap (p. 128) and Green Gable (p. 40).

The local organisation for the sport is the *Fell and Rock Climbing Club*. Their Journal publishes the authoritative guides to the Rock Climbing in the District: "*Pillar Rock*"; "*Scafell Group*"; "*Great Gable*"; "*Borrowdale*"; "*Buttermere and Newlands*"; "*Dow Crag*"; "*Longdale*" *and* "*Eastern Fells.*"

Good books on rock-mountaineering in the Lake District are *Rock Climbing in the English Lake District*, by O. G. Jones (3rd edition, edited by George and Ashley P. Abraham); *Crag and Hound in Lakeland*, and *British Mountaineering*, by C. E. Benson; and *Teach Yourself Mountain Climbing*, by G. Francis.

Sailing

Windermere is the headquarters for sailing, though the sport is also followed on some of the other lakes. Motor-boating is, of course, very popular. The caution with regard to squalls given under Boating (p. 17) is re-emphasised with tenfold force in regard to sailing.

Sports Meetings

A popular feature of the Lakeland season are the Sports Meetings and other similar gatherings, of which the most famous is the **Grasmere Sports,** usually on the third Thursday in August. This meeting is notable for a very stiff Fell Race to the top of Butter Crags and back; it is also the *locus classicus* for the Cumberland and Westmorland style of wrestling. Sheep-Dog Trials take place on Applethwaite Common, near Windermere, Rydal, Keswick, Patterdale and elsewhere. None of these meetings is complete without a *Hound Trail*, spectacular events peculiar to this part of England.

Tennis

There are public tennis courts at Windermere, Ambleside, Keswick, Coniston, Penrith, Kendal, Grange-over-Sands, etc., which may be hired by the hour at reasonable charges. In most cases there are both hard and grass courts.

Winter Sports

When, as not infrequently happens, the lakes are frozen over (with the exception of Wastwater, which is never completely covered), grand skating is to be had, especially on the shallower lakes, Derwentwater, Rydal, Esthwaite and Tarn Hows. Curling is a favourite sport at Keswick, and those who are not acquainted with the "roaring game" may have an opportunity of learning something of its fascination and difficulty. Ski-ing is frequently enjoyed, but those who follow this exhilarating pastime are warned that runs often terminate in abrupt, craggy declivities. They will also find that the innumerable stone walls may be a danger as well as an impediment. The best slopes are on the Helvellyn, Skiddaw and High Street ranges of fells, as these are less broken and rocky than the fells in the centre of the district where only the expert can ski safely. Snow conditions vary greatly from season to season.

The Lake District National Park

In May 1951 some 866 sq. miles of the Lake district became a National Park. It is thus marked out as one of Britain's finest scenic areas: a national asset to be defended against threats of spoliation and to be preserved for the enjoyment of the nation.

The administration of the National Park falls to the Lake District Planning Board who, as the Planning Authority for the area, are charged with seeing that all applications to develop land are controlled with appropriate high standards in order to preserve its natural beauty. But besides this, under the general supervision of the Countryside Commission, they are to take measures to enhance still further the natural beauty of the area and to improve, where necessary, its facilities for recreational enjoyment. They may, for example, take action to remove unsightly buildings, improve unsightly land, preserve or plant trees; make arrangements for the provision of accommodation, meals and refreshments, camping sites, and parking places; and arrange facilities for sailing, boating, bathing and fishing. The Planning Board have already completed several of these "improving" actions and have others in hand.

It is important that all should understand that within the National Park the normal life of the people who live and work there still goes on as usual. Designation does not change the ownership of land: the land is not nationalised. Moreover, no additional public right of access over land is conferred. Much of the fells is open to visitors, but tracks and footpaths, as elsewhere in the countryside, pass through private property or across the farmer's land. And when enjoying the beauty of the Lakeland scene with its great variety of plant and animal life and many other attractions, visitors—walkers, cyclists, motorists and picnickers alike—should be mindful of their responsibilities to help preserve its beauty for the enjoyment of themselves and others, do no damage, keep to the paths across farmland, fasten all gates, leave no litter and otherwise remember the ten simple maxims for good country behaviour in the Country Code prepared by the Countryside Commission.

Much of the National Park area is in the safeguarding hands of the National Trust. And those who cherish and enjoy the lakeland scene also owe much to the Friends of the Lake District (who operate from Pennington near Ulverston) and to the Council for the Preservation of Rural England, who have fought so vigorously for its preservation.

HISTORICAL SKETCH

The early history of the Lake Counties has been powerfully influenced by its geography. The high central mass of country now so eagerly sought by the tourist was always very scantily populated, the chief centres of population being the Eden valley, the Cumberland coast, Furness and Cartmel, and the fertile valleys of the Kent and Lune. Many of the valley bottoms remained undrained till recent times and houses were generally built on the lower hill slopes.

From about 1800 B.C. various streams of invaders penetrated the Lake Counties, principally from the Eden Valley and the sea coast. Their most impressive memorials are the great stone circles such as "Long Meg" and that at Keswick, their most numerous the implements of stone and metal which have frequently been found in most corners of the district. The Roman conquest of Cumberland and Westmorland began about A.D. 80. Important Roman roads connected *inter alia* Stainmoor with Brougham, Low Borrow Bridge (near Tebay) with Carlisle, Brougham and Ambleside and Ravenglass (over Hardknott and Wrynose) and Carlisle with Papcastle and Maryport. Roman Lakeland was always a military area with civilisation confined largely to the forts: outside these the natives lived in rude embanked settlements (many of which can still be traced on the fells).

From about A.D. 600 Lakeland was gradually absorbed in the great Anglian kingdom of Northumbria. Carlisle and Cartmel were given to St. Cuthbert; monasteries sprang up as at Dacre and Heversham and the artistic renaissance of the time has left memorials in the earlier fragments of cross shafts still to be found in some of the churches of Lakeland. In the first years of the tenth century began the devastating Viking raids, some originating from the Danish kingdom of York, others from Ireland and the Isle of Man. The impression they left was profound and permanent. The dialect and traditions of Lakeland are largely Scandinavian and the memory of these invaders is imperishably preserved in such place-name terminations as -thwaite, -saetr, -erg, and -by.

In the confusion of the times the Lake Counties became a no-man's-land between Scotland and England and by the time of the Norman Conquest the Eden valley and north Cumberland were held by the Scottish king. But in 1092 William Rufus took Carlisle and in the following decades Lakeland was gradually welded into the English kingdom. Throughout the Middle Ages it suffered from almost incessant Scottish raids; these were the principal motive for the erection of the stone "pele" towers, many of which remain, sometimes embedded in later houses. Larger castles lay mainly along the Eden valley at Brough, Appleby, Brougham and Carlisle, but substantial remains are also found at Naworth, Cockermouth, Egremont and Kendal. Medieval monasteries were few here, for the country was sparsely populated and far from rich, but important relics of houses exist at Carlisle, Calder, Cartmel, Furness and Lanercost.

With the union of England and Scotland (1603) peace at last descended, and coupled with the steady growth of sheep farming, led to a steady rise to prosperity. Farmhouses with their prominent round chimneys spread farther up the fellsides and by the end of the century much fine furniture was being produced locally. The Civil War caused some disturbance principally at Carlisle which suffered a long siege and no little damage in 1644–5.

The Jacobites entered the district in their dismal revolts of 1715 and 1745 and in December of the latter year occurred their rearguard action at Clifton near Penrith, which has been termed "the last battle on English soil."

The later eighteenth century was a placid period and is mainly notable for the first signs of the great tide of tourists. The poet Gray visited Lakeland in 1767 and 1769, and in the following generation a number of the first important guide-books to the district were published. In the "eighteen forties" the foundation of the present railway system had been laid, making the future problem of Lakeland not how to visit it but how to preserve it.

A Note on Geology

Broadly speaking the rocks of the Lake District proper are divided into three wide bands trending ENE–WSW. The oldest of these, known as the Skiddaw Slates, is a thick group of bluish-grey to black sandy clay-slates found north of a line from Troutbeck Station, Cumberland, to Egremont. They are the worn-down core of a mountain range that arose from the crumpling of this part of the earth's crust into a complex arch. Newer rocks laid down above these beds before the folding are now found to the south of this axial core. They are the green, grey and purplish lavas and volcanic ashes (including the well-known green roofing slates) of the Borrowdale Volcanic Series. These hard, well-jointed or, in places, sheared slaty rocks form the rugged central mountains from Ullswater to Wastwater. South of a line from Shap Wells to Millom the younger

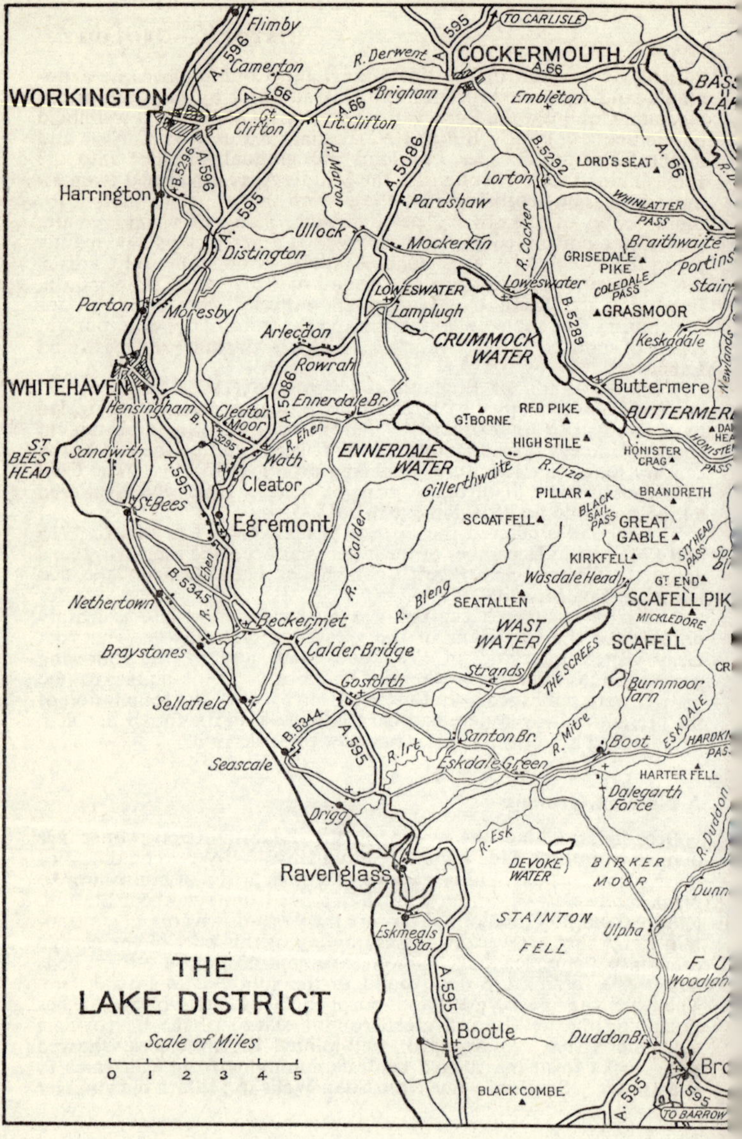
THE
LAKE DISTRICT
Scale of Miles
0 1 2 3 4 5
WORKINGTON
COCKERMOUTH
WHITEHAVEN
Egremont
Cleator
Ravenglass
Bootle
Flimby
Camerton
Harrington
Distington
Parton
Moresby
Hensingham
Sandwith
ST. BEES HEAD
St. Bees
Nethertown
Braystones
Sellafield
Seascale
Drigg
Eskmeals Sta.
Beckermet
Calder Bridge
Gosforth
Santon Br.
Eskdale Green
Boot
Dalegarth Force
Ulpha
Duddon Br.
Cleator Moor
Wath
Arlecdon
Rowrah
Ennerdale Br.
Ullock
Mockerkin
Pardshaw
Brigham
Gt Clifton
Lit. Clifton
Embleton
Lorton
Loweswater
LOWESWATER
Lamplugh
CRUMMOCK WATER
Buttermere
BUTTERMERE
ENNERDALE WATER
Gillerthwaite
WAST WATER
THE SCREES
Strands
Wasdale Head
Burnmoor Tarn
DEVOKE WATER
BIRKER MOOR
STAINTON FELL
BLACK COMBE
LORD'S SEAT
WHINLATTER PASS
Braithwaite
GRISEDALE PIKE
COLEDALE PASS
GRASMOOR
Keskadale
Newlands
RED PIKE
GT. BORNE
HIGH STILE
HONISTER CRAG
HONISTER PASS
PILLAR
BLACK SAIL PASS
BRANDRETH
GREAT GABLE
KIRKFELL
SCOAT FELL
SEATALLEN
STY HEAD PASS
GT. END
SCAFELL PIKE
MICKLEDORE
SCAFELL
ESKDALE
HARTER FELL
R. Derwent
R. Marron
R. Cocker
R. Ehen
R. Calder
R. Bleng
R. Liza
R. Irt
R. Mitre
R. Esk
R. Duddon
TO CARLISLE
TO BARROW
A. 595
A. 596
A. 66
A. 5086
B. 5296
B. 5292
B. 5289
B. 5295
B. 5345
B. 5344

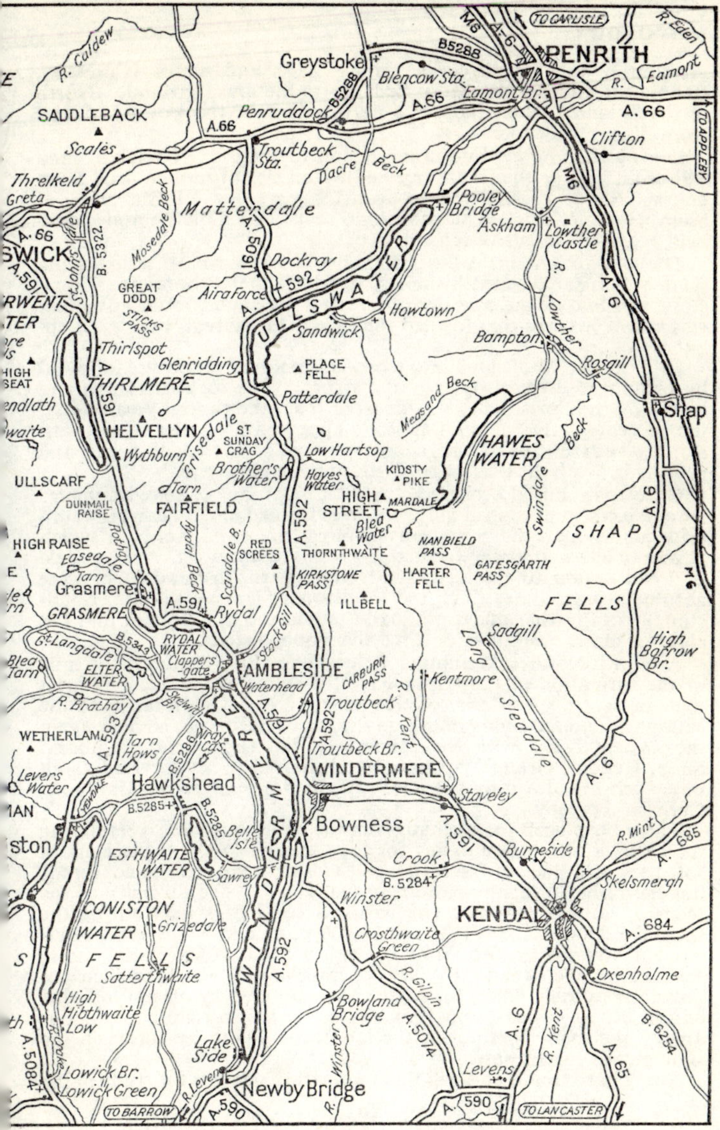
TO CARLISLE
PENRITH
R. Eden
R. Eamont
Greystoke
B5288
Blencow Sta.
Eamont Br.
A.66
R. Caldew
SADDLEBACK
Scales
Penruddock
Troutbeck Sta.
Clifton
TO APPLEBY
Threlkeld
Greta
Matterdale
Dacre Beck
Pooley Bridge
Askham
Lowther Castle
M6
SWICK
B. 5322
St John's Vale
Mosedale Beck
A.5091
Dockray
A.591
GREAT DODD
STICKS PASS
Aira Force
A.592
ULLSWATER
Howtown
R. Lowther
A.6
Thirlspot
Sandwick
Bampton
Rosgill
HIGH SEAT
THIRLMERE
Glenridding
PLACE FELL
Patterdale
Measand Beck
Shap
HELVELLYN
Grisedale
ST SUNDAY CRAG
HAWES WATER
Wythburn
Low Hartsop
Brother's Water
Hayes Water
KIDSTY PIKE
Swindale Beck
ULLSCARF
DUNMAIL RAISE
Tarn
FAIRFIELD
HIGH STREET
MARDALE
Blea Water
SHAP
HIGH RAISE
Easedale Tarn
Rothay
Rydal Beck
Scandale B.
RED SCREES
THORNTHWAITE
NAN BIELD PASS
GATESGARTH PASS
Grasmere
KIRKSTONE PASS
HARTER FELL
ILL BELL
FELLS
GRASMERE
A.591
Rydal
Stock Gill
Long Sleddale
Sadgill
High Borrow Br.
Gt. Langdale
B.5343
RYDAL WATER
Blea Tarn
ELTER WATER
Clappersgate
AMBLESIDE
Waterhead
CARBURN PASS
Kentmore
R. Brathay
Skelwith Br.
Troutbeck
R. Kent
WETHERLAM
A.593
Tarn Hows
B.5286
Wray Cas.
Troutbeck Br.
Levers Water
Hawkshead
WINDERMERE
Staveley
YEWDALE
B.5285
Bowness
R. Mint
A.685
ston
Belle Isle
ESTHWAITE WATER
Sawrey
Crook
Burneside
B. 5284
Skelsmergh
Winster
CONISTON WATER
Grizedale
KENDAL
A.684
Crosthwaite Green
FELLS
Satterthwaite
Oxenholme
High Hibthwaite
Low
Bowland Bridge
R. Gilpin
B. 6254
A.5074
R. Crake
Lake Side
R. Winster
A.65
A.5084
Lowick Br.
Lowick Green
R. Leven
Newby Bridge
Levens
A.590
TO BARROW
TO LANCASTER

green-grey and purple grits, sandy flags and slates (Coniston, Bannisdale and Kirkby Moor beds) form the lower ground. North of the Skiddaw Slates there is a narrow strip of the Volcanic Series from Binsey to Berrier.

During the arching and compression of these "Ordovician" and "Silurian" rocks they were injected by masses of molten rock from below. These crystallised to form the granitic "intrusions" of Shap, Eskdale, etc. (The roadstone rocks of Embleton and Threlkeld are also "intrusive igneous rocks.")

The old mountains were gradually worn down to a low-lying plain which sank beneath the sea in which the carboniferous limestone was laid down, and upon the latter the sands, muds and great vegetation swamps that formed the "Coal Measures" were accumulated.

Uplift of the whole area into a broad, fractured dome was followed by prolonged erosion by rain and rivers. The rocks down to and including the limestone were removed from the central part so that the truncated edge of the limestone appeared as a ring of outward sloping beds enclosing the central region of the older rocks and passing beneath the coal-bearing strata at its outer rim.

Once again burial occurred. At first great fans of rock fragments from the resistant central hill-mass were formed under desert or semi-arid conditions on the margins of areas of saline water in which gypsum beds were being formed in the south and west. In the Vale of Eden region to the east, sand dunes (Penrith Sandstone) were accumulating. Later thick red sandstones (Triassic St. Bees Sandstone) from farther afield gradually buried the central area and red clays or marls eventually covered the whole district.

After a long interval another dome-like uplift—at about the time of the formation of the Alps—gave the rocks of the Lake District their present disposition. Active stream erosion soon removed the soft marls and red sandstone from the top of the dome; so once again the ancient rocks with their limestone rim (Egrement, Caldbeck, Shap, Kendal, Grange) appeared and the red rocks survived as an outer belt low down on the flanks of the dome (Barrow, Maryport, Carlisle, Appleby).

There have been many changes in the courses of the rivers during the carving of hill and valley for they selectively chose the belts of soft rock and lines of fracturing as these were gradually uncovered; but the radial drainage pattern has survived. The diversity of the scenery, however, owes much to the action of glaciers during the Glacial Period, some 600,000 to 20,000 years ago. The great semi-circular coombs or cirques at the valley heads (Bleaberry Coomb, Red Tarn), the broad "U" shaped valleys with the lake-filled depressions in their floors (in some cases dammed by glacial moraine and in others "rock-basins" excavated by the ice) are conspicuous among the many features of the landscape due to ice-action in the geologically recent past.

Many have found and will find fascinating subjects for study in the rocks and their fossils, in the minerals of the old mine workings and in gaining an appreciation of the forces of nature which shaped the wonderful variety of the hills and the dales.

References: Northern England (*Regional Guide, Memoir of the Geological Survey*), gives a simple general account of the geology of the district, and a more advanced but readable book is Marr's *Geology of the Lake District* (Cambridge University Press).

Natural History

The Lake District, from its natural configuration, the lengthy and varied sweep of coast from Morecambe Bay to Whitehaven, with many beautiful river and beck estuaries; its richly wooded valleys and sheltered streams; its large and smaller lakes and meres and lonely tarns; its high and rugged mountains and great stretches of upland fell-land, was naturally at one time perhaps richer than any other part of England in the number and variety of its fauna. Happily it is even yet, in many parts, still well favoured in that respect, and the Wild Birds Protection Acts have restored the district to something of its ancient glory by reducing the destruction of many rare, beautiful, and useful birds.

There are but few works now in print which deal with Nature in Lakeland. The best Natural History is H. A. Macpherson's *The Vertebrate Fauna of Lakeland*; birds are well dealt with in the works of the late Miss M. L. Armitt, and in *The Birds of Lakeland*, published by the Carlisle Natural History Society. *A Flora of the English Lake District*, by J. G. Baker, though probably obtainab e only from the larger reference libraries, is admirable and concise.

The birds of the Lake Country number 262 species, according to Mr. Macpherson. This is four more than the number recorded for Lancashire, and forty more than the best authorities give to Cheshire. The Lake District is able to list rather more rare and accidental visitors than can its neighbours, but the winter birds are somewhat fewer in number. Several species entirely depart with the approach of winter, when the uplands become impossible for bird-life.

Once the central mountains contained a richer and more distinctive fauna than now, but they still have wild life worth noticing. The peregrine falcon, though harried almost to extinction by collectors, nests on the loftiest and remotest precipices. The buzzard and raven are not so rare as has been stated; the kestrel holds its own, as does the well-hunted sparrow-hawk; so does the merlin on the lower moors.

Of the mammals of Lakeland, beyond the weasel, the squirrel, the hedgehog and mice, little is seen. But if the visitor rambles from Ullswater into some of the loneliest recesses of the mountains he may meet with the native red deer, still wild. He may find the earth (locally "whoal" or "bield") of the fox high up, and the holt of the otter by the secluded shore of the lake, but he is little likely to catch a glimpse of either of these cautious creatures. The pine marten and foumart are very rare and most unlikely to be seen; the badger, on the other hand, is by no means extinct.

As might be expected from an area showing so much variety in its rock formation, Lakeland is the favourite haunt of many species of butterflies and moths, some of which are rarely, if at all, found elsewhere in England. Some of the mountain insects are considered great prizes by the entomologist, *Erebias epiphron* in particular. This species is abundant at high elevations in Lakeland, never being seen below 2,000 feet, where only a stray white or tortoiseshell or the ubiquitous *pamphilus* bear it company. Above that limit they may be seen in scores; 200 feet lower you may look in vain for a stray specimen. But the day must be well chosen, for the dark little fellow delights in sunshine. He is not to be found again between Red Screes and the Alps, where he may be met with at about 4,000 or 5,000 feet.

LAKELAND TERMS AND THEIR MEANINGS

Band: A long ridge dividing two areas of less elevation.

Barrow: A hill.

Beck: Stream generally, but more often applied to mountain torrents.

Bent: Coarse fell grass.

Bield: A shelter. In fox hunting it signifies a fastness in the rocks inaccessible to hounds.

Bink: A grassy ledge on a precipitous face; often used as a refuge by foxes.

Blea: In dialect and place-name alike the word means "cold blue."

Borran: A heap of stones or broken rocks.

Brant: Steep.

Burn: Probably the same word as *Borran.* It does not appear to mean brook.

Cairn: A pile of stones, generally erected to mark the way, or to denote the summit of a fell.

Cam: The ridge of a hill, or of a portion of a hill.

Den: A valley.

Dodd: An elevated point, a dependency of the main fell, *e.g.* Stybarrow Dodd, Watson's Dodd and Great Dodd on Helvellyn. The summit is generally rounded.

Dore: An opening between walls of rocks. The Great Dore, Mickledore, is between Scafell Pikes and Scafell, two mountains.

Dub: A river pool.

Dun: A dune or down.

Fell: A term generally used for the mountains, but also applied to common lands of no great elevation.

Force: A waterfall.

Garth, Gard and Guard: Enclosed piece of land of small size.

Gate: A way. These words occur in conjunction at Gatesgarth, near Buttermere, "the enclosure by the way."

Ghyll (or Gill): A narrow ravine or gully through which a mountain stream runs. Some of the most beautiful Lakeland scenery is found in the less savage ghylls.

Grain: (a prong): the fork of a stream.

Grise: (a common prefix): Wild boar; *e.g.* Grisedale.

Hag: A wood; enclosed ground.

Hause: The summit of a pass (a *col*).

Heaf: A mountain sheep pasture.

Holme: An island.

How: A rounded elevation; a hill.

Intack: An enclosure on a fell side generally surrounded by stone walls.

Kell, Keld: A spring or well, found in place-names such as Gunnerkeld, Threlkeld, etc.

Knock: A hill.

Knott: A rocky excrescence on a hill— a "knotted" hill. Hardknott, Hanging Knott, etc.

Knowe: A rounded hill.

Lath: A barn.

Man (Celtic, "mawn"): A cairn on a summit, or marking a route. Not necessarily the highest point of the mass. The terms High Man and Low Man are not uncommon.

Mere: A lake.

Nab: A promontory, a projection, an extremity.

Ness: (a nose): A projection, not necessarily into a lake.

Pike: A prominent peak on the fells—Pike o' Stickle, etc.

Pitch: An abrupt ascent.

Raise: The summit of a ridge; a heap of stones.

Rake: A natural vertical or diagonal passage on the face of a cliff affording a way to the top; the fundamental idea being "reach."

Rigg: A ridge.

Scale: A rough hut; a shieling.

Scarth: A frontage of rocks on a fell side; a notch in a ridge.

Scree: A bank of loose stones lying at a high angle; the debris of cliffs.

Sike: A rivulet in marshy ground.

Slack: A slight depression between two elevations.

Slape: Smooth, slippery.

Spout: A waterfall.

Stickle: A sharp peak.

Tarn: A small mountain lake.

Thwaite: A clearing.

Walla: Sad-coloured, grey.

Wath: A ford—Sandwath, Yanwath, etc.

Wray: A landmark.

Wyke: A bay.

Dimensions of Lakes

The figures on following pages are necessarily only approximate. The dimensions of the lakes, of course, fluctuate according to rainfall, and in the case of Thirlmere and Haweswater are dependent on the needs of Manchester. Even a slight rise of water may increase the acreage of the lake considerably.

In flood-time so copious are the mountain becks that whole dale-troughs become temporary lakes, and the low-lying ground between Buttermere and Crummock, and between Derwentwater and Bassenthwaite, is entirely submerged. In the latter case, a new lake extends from Grange Bridge in Borrowdale down to Ouse Bridge on the Derwent, a dozen miles of uninterrupted waterway.

Lakes.	Length. (In miles.)	Breadth. (In miles.)	Depth. (In feet.)	Elevation (In feet.)
Windermere	10½	1¼	219	130
Ullswater	7½	¾	205	476
Coniston	5¼	½	184	143
Bassenthwaite	4	¾	70	223
*Thirlmere	3½	½	158	533
Derwentwater	3	1⅛	72	244
Wastwater	3	½	258	200
Crummock Water	2½	⅝	144	321
Ennerdale Water	2½	¾	148	368
†Haweswater	4½	½	198	790
Esthwaite Water	1½	⅜	80	217
Loweswater	1¼	⅜	60	429
Buttermere	1¼	⅜	94	329
Grasmere	1	½	75	208
Rydal Water	¾	¼	55	181
Brothers' Water	⅜	¼	70	520

* Original acreage, 330 statute acres. As at first raised, 20 feet, 565 acres; length, 3¼ miles; breadth, 700 yards. As now raised, 50 feet; length, 3½ miles (to beyond Wythburn); breadth ½ mile.

† The old lake had a length of 2½ miles and a breadth of ⅜ mile.

Elterwater is 187 feet above sea-level. It is so disconnected in construction that it is impossible to estimate other measurements with accuracy.

Heights of Passes

Where possible, the mountain dominating the pass is quoted to aid identification. Where this cannot be done, prominent features on the map are quoted with the same object.

Pass	Feet.
[1]Esk Hause (Great End)	2,490
Sticks Pass (Raise and Stybarrow Dodd, Helvellyn)	2,420
Windy Gap (between Pillar and Steeple)	2,200
Nan Bield Pass (Harter Fell, High Street)	2,100
Greenup Edge (between High Raise and Ullscarf)	1,995
Walna Scar (Brown Pike, Coniston)	1,990
Gatescarth (Branstree, Harter Fell)	1,950
Grisedale (Fairfield, Seat Sandal, Dollywaggon Pike)	1,929
Black Sail (Kirkfell and Pillar Fell)	1,800
Scandale Head (Red Screes and Dove Crag)	1,700
Sty Head (Great Gable)	1,600

Stake Pass [between Langdale and Langstrath (Langdale Pikes)]	1,576
Kirkstone (Red Screes)	1,476
Garburn (Kentmere to Troutbeck, Windermere, South of Ill Bell)	1,450
Scarf Gap (High Crag and Buttermere Haystacks)	1,400
Floutern (Great Borne and Gavel Fell)	1,300
Hardknott [Duddon Valley and Eskdale (Bowfell)]	1,290
Wrynose [Little Langdale and Duddon Valley (Pike o' Blisco and Wetherlam)]	1,270
Honister [Rosthwaite to Buttermere (Grey Knotts and Dale Head)]	1,190
Buttermere Hause to Newlands (Robinson)	1,096
Whinlatter (Grisedale Pike and Lorton Fells)	1,043
Dunmail Raise [Thirlmere and Grasmere (Seat Sandal and Steel Fell)]	782

[1] The elevation of Esk Hause is generally given at about 100 feet lower, *i.e.* the summit of the pass from Langdale to Wasdale. To reach Eskdale it is, however, necessary to cross the real summit of the hause.

Points 2,000 feet and upwards above Sea-level

There is always room for diversity on this head. In all cases we have done our best to give the exact height of each elevation. It may be taken as read that the discrepancies, if any, do not amount to more than a very few feet.

For convenience we have divided the Fells into groups readily recognisable having an elevation of 2,000 feet or over.

(*a*) Skiddaw and Saddleback Group

	Feet.		Feet.
Skiddaw	3,053	Scales Fell	2,203
Saddleback	2,847	Dead Crags	2,189
Skiddaw, Low Man	2,837	Carrock Fell (*N.E. Bowscale Fell*)	2,173
Gate Ghyll Fell	2,500	Bannerdale Crags	2,100
Carlside	2,400	Comb Height (*N. Great Calva*)	2,058
Lonscale Fell	2,344	High Pike (*N.E. Great Calva*)	2,000
Bowscale Fell	2,306		
Great Calva	2,265		
Ullock Pike	2,230		

(*b*) Grassmoor Group

Grassmoor	2,791	Sand Hill	2,450
Eel Crags	2,749	Whiteside	2,317
Grisedale Pike	2,593	Scar Crags	2,205
Wandhope	2,533	Whiteless Pike	2,159
Hopegill Head or Hobcarton Pike	2,525	Hobcarton End	2,010
Sail	2,530	Causey Pike	2,000

(*c*) Buttermere Group

High Stile	2,643	Starling Dodd	2,085
Red Pike	2,479	Great Borne	2,019
High Crag	2,443		

(*d*) Pillar Group

Pillar	2,927	Caw Fell (*S. Iron Crag*)	2,188
Scoatfell	2,760	Iron Crag	2,071
Red Pike	2,707	Looking Stead	2,058
Steeple	2,687	Yewbarrow	2,058
Haycock	2,619	Tewit How	2,014
Little Gowder Crag	2,410	Stirrup Crag	2,009
Seatallan	2,266		

(*e*) Scafell Group

Scafell Pike (Summit of England)	3,210	Glaramara	2,560
Scafell	3,162	Stonesty Pike	2,544
Broad Crag	3,054	Slight Side	2,501
Ill Crag	3,040	Hanging Knott	2,500
Great End	2,984	Red How	2,426
Bowfell	2,960	Pike o' Blisco	2,304
Long Pike	2,940	Cold Pike	2,259
[1]Esk Pike	2,903	High House, Seathwaite Fell (ap.)	2,250
Crinkle Crags (Long Top)	2,816	Great Knott	2,150
Black Crag	2,689	Harter Fell	2,140
Shelter Crags	2,667	Yeastyrigg Crags (ap.)	2,050
Lingmell	2,649	Rosthwaite (or Chapel) Fell	2,000
Allen Crags	2,572		

1 Generally incorrectly known as Hanging Knott, a shoulder of Bowfell which overhangs Angle Tarn. The old original name was Tongue Head.

(*f*) Great Gable Group

Great Gable	2,949	Greyknotts	2,287
Green Gable	2,643	Fleetwith Pike	2,126
Kirkfell	2,631	Base Brown	2,120
Kirkfell Crags	2,579	Honister Crag	2,070
Brandreth	2,344		

(*g*) Newlands Group

Dale Head	2,473	Scawdel Fell	2,143
Robinson	2,417	Knitting How (ap.)	2,100
Hindscarth	2,385		

(*h*) High Raise Group

High Raise	2,500	Thunacar Knott	2,351
Sergeant Man	2,414	Pike o' Stickle	2,323
Harrison Stickle	2,403	Pavey Ark	2,288
*High White Stones	2,374	Greenup	2,080
Ullscarf	2,370	Coldbarrow Fell	2,050

* There is some confusion as to these points, some cartographers having mistaken High White Stones, a "trig" point selected by the Ordnance Survey, for the summit of the fell.

(*i*) Helvellyn Group†

Helvellyn	3,118	Hartside	2,481
Helvellyn Low Man	3,033	Seat Sandal	2,415
Nethermost Pike (Birkside)	2,920	Whelpside	2,412
Catchedicam	2,917	Clough Head	2,380
Raise	2,889	Tarn Crag	2,370
Fairfield	2,863	Greenhow End	2,360
Striding Edge	2,832	Birkhouse Moor and Glenridding Common	2,318
Browncove Crags	2,819	Raven Crag (Red Screes)	2,280
Dollywaggon Pike	2,810	Whiteside (ap.)	2,250
Great Dodd	2,807	Calfhow Pike	2,166
Stybarrow Dodd	2,767	Scandale Fell	2,166
St. Sunday Crag	2,756	Stang	2,149
Hart Crag	2,698	Middle Dodd	2,106
Dove Crag	2,603	Wanthwaite Fell (ap.)	2,190
Watson's Dodd	2,584	Snarker Pike	2,096
Gavel Pike	2,577	Little Hart Crag	2,061
Red Screes	2,541	Rydal Fell	2,022
Great Rigg	2,513		
Cofa Pike	2,500		

† Grisedale Pass does not appear a sufficiently definite break to warrant the division of this section into Helvellyn and Fairfield Ranges. As a practical range these fells are continuous.

(*k*) High Street Group

High Street	2,718	Yoke	2,292
High Raise	2,634	Gray Crag	2,286
Harter Fell	2,585	Rest Dodd	2,278
Rampsgill Head	2,581	Loadpot Hill	2,201
Thornthwaite Cra	2,569	Low Rise	2,191
Kidsty Pike	2,560	Lingmell End	2,183
The Knowe	2,509	Adam Seat	2,180
Caudale Moor (Stony Cove Pike)	2,502	High Kop	2,179
Mardale Ill Bell	2,496	Tarn Crag (Longsleddale)	2,176
Ill Bell	2,476	Weather Hill	2,174
John Bell's Banner	2,474	Place Fell	2,154
Whelter Crags	2,465	Raven Crag	2,150
The Knott	2,423	Selside Pike	2,142
Kentmere Pike	2,397	Rough Crag	2,062
Froswick	2,359	Harrop Pike	2,060
Raven How	2,358	Hart Hill	2,057
Branstree	2,333	Bleathwaite Crag	2,050
Red Crag	2,328	Lower Hartsop Dodd	2,018
		Gavel Crag	2,000

(*l*) Coniston Group

Old Man	2,635	Great How Crags	2,525
Swirl How	2,630	Wetherlam	2,502
Brim Fell	2,611	Brown Pike	2,239
Carrs	2,575	Walna Scar	2,035
Dow Crag	2,555	Lad Stones	2,019
Grey Friar	2,536		

Walking in Lakeland

Two Suggested Tours

The district is probably the finest touring ground for walkers in the entire country and there is ample freedom of access nearly everywhere. Certain tracks and footpaths pass through private property and walkers are asked not to stray into enclosed woods or fields adjacent to them. The fells are almost invariably open to anybody. On pp. 35–45 are given outlines of all the ordinary routes through the district; below are two specimen tours for a week-end or a fortnight.

A Week-end Tour

Saturday. From Windermere by bus to Tongue Ghyll (Grasmere) or Wythburn. From the former ascend Helvellyn by Grisedale Pass; from the latter by the ordinary route from Wythburn. Descend in either case to Thirlspot, from which walk to Keswick, or take the bus again.

Sunday afternoon. At Keswick. Walk to Rosthwaite or Seatoller in Borrowdale or continue to Buttermere by the Honister Pass.

Monday. From Rosthwaite or Seatoller by the Buttermere road to the quarry buildings of Honister Hause, thence by the "drum house" to Great Gable. From Buttermere ascend by Warnscale Bottom. Thence by Angle Tarn and Rossett Ghyll to Langdale, whence there is a frequent service of buses to Ambleside and Windermere.

A 14-day Tour

It is recommended that the walk begin from *Coniston*, but, of course, the round can be started at any point to suit.

1. Coniston to Windermere by Hawkshead and the Ferry.
2. Windermere to Patterdale by Ill Bell, Thornthwaite Crag and Hartsop.
3. Patterdale to Keswick by Helvellyn (last 8 miles by bus if preferred).
4. Keswick to Wastwater by Borrowdale and Great Gable (first 8 miles by bus if preferred).

5. Wastwater to Langdale by Scafell Pike, Esk Hause and Rossett Ghyll.
6. Langdale to Grasmere by the Pikes, Pavey Ark, and Easedale.
7. Grasmere to Ambleside by Fairfield and Scandale (for Windermere Station).

If the start is made from either Windermere or Keswick the next stage will be from Ambleside to Coniston, preferably by Barn Gates and Tarn Hows. Should the weather be wild or there is mist on the tops, the route from Patterdale to Keswick may be taken by the Grisedale Pass, from Keswick to Wasdale by the Styhead, from Wastwater to Langdale by Burnmoor and the Hardknott and Wrynose Passes.

Several days are left, which will be all too easily filled by other mountain ascents. The best expedition is, to our mind, the traverse of the Buttermere Fells from Scale Force to Scarf Gap. Others we would specially recommend are Grassmoor from Keswick, Pillar Fell from Wasdale, Bowfell from Langdale, or the round of the Coniston Fells, ascending by the Old Man and returning to Coniston by Wetherlam.

WALKING ROUTES

A General Outline Guide

For the first few mountain ascents it is advisable to take a companion or two. A map and a compass should always be carried. Stout nailed boots should be worn. The ascents described can be used as descents and *vice versa*, according to the point from which the start is made (of course, instructions for turning right or left must be interpreted correspondingly). Descents marked (A) are good alternative routes of ascent. *Arêtes* (narrow ridges) should be avoided in wet or windy weather, especially if the wind is blowing in gusts. In mists it is better to keep off the fells. Places noted as *steep, narrow*, etc., should be approached slowly. Violent exercise, even on level ground, often occasions giddiness; and many people experience for a time at any rate a feeling of wavering on ridges, or at the edge of precipices, which even slight temporary fatigue is likely to increase to a disagreeable and possibly dangerous degree. New-comers to the District should see the note on pp. 18–19 regarding the identification of tracks.

The arrangement of the fells in groups notified on p. 31 is adhered to. Only the principal lines of ascent are dealt with particularly. Those who follow the other routes here indicated, and especially adventurous spirits who are disposed to disregard recognised tracks, are warned that crags and precipices abound, that they very often form the unexpectedly abrupt termination of upward slopes, and that a fall of 30 feet is generally as effective as one of 300. It is sound advice to follow the watersheds. The Helvellyn, Great Gable and High Street groups are peculiarly favourable to this mode of travelling. **R** = right; **L** = left.

For details as to views, etc., *see* the sub-section **Fells,** at the end of each of the Southern, Northern and Eastern sections into which the book is divided.

(*a*) Skiddaw and Saddleback Group (*see* p. 102)

With Carrock, Bowscale, and Lonscale Fells, Carlside, Great Calva and Ullock Pike. The travelling throughout is generally easy. Many precipices on Saddleback.

Skiddaw. From Keswick. Pass under railway station. Turn **L** to lane with signpost "To Skiddaw"; then **R** up lane to gate (just short of this an enclosed path **R** leads to Latrigg); **R** through another gate; **L** through another gate and on upwards; where the wall bends **R**, turn **R** and then **L** at once (the path **R** leads to Lonscale Fell). Continue over shoulder and along Keswick edge of plateau. Leave Low Man **L**, skirting base, and follow unmistakable path to High Man.

Descents. To Keswick. Reverse route of ascent, or from S. point of High Man, down ridge to summit of Carlside, thence to Millbeck hamlet, keeping as nearly as possible in line with west side of Derwentwater. Scree (very steep) and some rock.

Saddleback. From Threlkeld *via* Scales village. From inn at Scales follow path over E. shoulder of Scales Fell, inclining **L** continually till Scales Tarn is **R**, then go straight up grass slope. Crags and precipices at both ends of saddle worth viewing.

Descents. Anywhere down grass slope towards Lonscale Fell inclining **L** (A). The upper track along valley (fine views) leads to Threlkeld village direct. The lower close by beck, also to Threlkeld, for Keswick, *via* Brundholme Woods, turning off at Derwent folds.

(*b*) **Grassmoor Group** (*see* p. 101)

Grassmoor, Eel Crag, Sail, Scar Crags, Sand Hill, Hobcarton, Hopegill Head, Whiteside, Grisedale, Whiteless and Causey Pikes. Travelling generally easy. Some narrow ridges.

Grassmoor from Braithwaite. Pass through village and take first fell path **L** on Whinlatter Road with Grisedale Pike **R**, skirting base. Ascend Force Crag (*steep*), with Crag **R**. Inclining slightly **R** reach top of Coledale Pass. Then turn **L** along stream to near source and climb Grassmoor **R.** Visit all points of plateau, as the views are unsurpassed. In returning by this route, keep Force Crag **L.** Grassmoor may be easily combined in an excursion with Grisedale Pike (*see* below).

Return. To Newlands Vale for Braithwaite and Keswick. From source of stream turn **L,** instead of **R** as for Grassmoor (above), over Eel Crag, down steep ridge over narrow ridges by Sail and Scar Crags to Causey Pike. Descent from Causey over Rowling End steep. An alternative is to return to Scar Crags and drop down grass slope **R,** *i.e.* west, on to old cart-track between Causey and Outerside.

To **Buttermere.** Starting with Grassmoor **R** and Eel Crag **L,** cross narrow ridge and descend Whiteless Pike (steep; path marked on map slightly **L** of Pike, but it is better to keep Pike **L**).

To **Scale Hill** (Cockermouth road; Crummock Water). From top of Coledale Pass descend rough path by ghyll between Grassmoor and Whiteside (A).

Grisedale Pike. From Braithwaite, second fell path **L** on Whinlatter Road. From shoulder (Kinn) keep to outside ridge. Final ascent steep, top narrow. Wall and wire fence lead to Sand Hill. View Hobcarton Crags, **R,** and descend **L** to Coledale Pass. From this point Grassmoor may be easily ascended (*see* above).

Scale Hill may be reached by continuing from Sand Hill over the narrow ridge of Whiteside, ending in a steep, rough descent.

(*c*) **Buttermere Group** (*see* p. 103)

High Crag, High Stile, Red Pike, with Starling Dodd, and Great Borne, with Melbreak. Hen Comb and outlying fells.

Travelling on the three principal fells somewhat rough. Upper ridge is precipitous towards Buttermere.

Red Pike from Buttermere village. Leave hotels **R,** cross bridge, turn **L** to Sour Milk Ghyll, ascend **L** by well-marked path to first ridge, turn **R** sharp along wood to Bleaberry Tarn (which may be reached direct by way of ghyll; the climb is stiff); incline **R** up screes to Red Pike.

Descents. It is best to return by the line of ascent. The Ruddy Beck descent is very steep and rough.

To Scale Force, Crummock Water. (A. This is the ascent from which to start the round of the Buttermere Fells.) From Pike with back to High Stile descend, inclining **R,** when a beck is reached. A wire fence is a useful guide. Last portion rather rough. The Force itself impracticable. Descent with Force **L** preferable.

To **Scarth Gap** for Gatesgarth. Follow ridge line by wire fence **L** from Pike above the tarn, over High Stile and High Crag, and by steep, rough descent to Scarf Gap, where turn **L** for Gatesgarth by well-marked path. Keep on the Ennerdale side of wire fence when on ridge line.

To **Gillerthwaite,** Ennerdale. With back to Red Pike and facing Ennerdale Lake, drop down slope (but *see* p. 120).

(*d*) Pillar Group (*see* p. 121)

Pillar Fell, Scoatfell, Steeple, Red Pike, Haycock, Yewbarrow, Looking Stead, with Seatallan. Travelling rough and in places difficult. Yewbarrow and Middlefell are both best left alone. Strangers should keep to walks.

Pillar Mountain from Wasdale Head. From summit of Black Sail Pass turn **L,** over Looking Stead, and keep ridge line by wire fence to summit. (Pillar Rock below **R.**) (*See also* pp. 121–122.) It is shorter but rather harder work to leave the Black Sail track near the head of Mosedale Valley, striking straight up Looking Stead.

Descents. Return to the summit of Blacksail Pass.

To Wasdale, *via* Scoatfell and Red Pike, from Windy Gap with back to Pillar. Incline **R** to skyline of Scoatfell, and then **L** along ridge line over Red Pike to Dore Head, when turn sharp **L** or incline **R** down either side of Yewbarrow *via* Overbeck or by a very steep scree shoot to Mosedale.

Scoatfell and Haycock and other fells.

Steeple itself is a conspicuous pointed spur projecting from Scoatfell into Ennerdale.

(*e*) Scafell Group (*see* p. 118)

Scafell Pike, Lingmell, Scafell, Great End, Bowfell, Crinkle Crags, Shelter Crags, Allen Crags, Glaramara, Seathwaite, Harter and Rosthwaite Fells, Pike o' Blisco. Travelling generally rough and even difficult. Strangers especially are advised not to leave the recognised tracks.

Esk Hause, the hub of the group is reached—(1) From Mickleden (head of Langdale) **L** from sheepfold by Rossett Ghyll Pass (bad), passing Angle Tarn and Esk Pike. (2) From Wasdale Head by Sty Head Pass (stony), passing Great End. (3) From Eskdale by following **R** branch of Esk from Esk Falls (right means, of course, proper right with regard to streams). (4) From Seathwaite by the Sty Head

Pass. (5) From Seathwaite by Grain Ghyll, cross to the **R** over Stockley Bridge, and then turn **L,** through gap in wall, passing between Seathwaite Fell and Glaramara. The Hause is an excellent place to make for in misty weather if astray on the Pikes, though in such conditions it is not an easy place from which to strike off any particular descent.

Bowfell from Langdale by Stool End Farm and so up ridge. The Band, between Oxendale and Mickleden: a rough finish may be avoided by a **L** turn below final rocks. From Eskdale. From Esk Falls follow the branch of the Esk, coming down on your right till the Three Tarns are in sight. Then **L** by cairned track. From Fell Foot, Little Langdale, by Wrynose Pass and Crinkle Crags. From head of Pass a little short of the Three Shire Stone **R** by line of cairns to summit of moor. Then **L** and climb over Cold Pike. Cross moor to Crinkle Crags which may be climbed or turned **L** (*see* p. 116. In any case turn second Crinkle **L**). Turn Shelter Crags **L** to the Three Tarns, whence cairns lead to summit. To be avoided in mist, as there are wide inter-spaces of moorland.

Descents to Langdale, Little Langdale and Eskdale. Closely follow lines of ascent.

From Esk Hause one may also reach:

Glaramara, best ascended from Rosthwaite, thus: From main road through gate just beyond Borrowdale Vicarage at the turning to Stonethwaite turn **L** with stream **R** to mill, inclining **R** by wood to foot of fell (here path from Seatoller and Thorneythwaite joins). Follow ridge line, choosing **R** side to head of combe, and thence to peaks (craggy). For Esk Hause continue S. by Allen Crags, over very rough ground (not to be attempted in mist). Both sides of fell precipitous, and for most of the way the fell provides uncomfortable going. Views very fine.

Descent to Borrowdale, reverse route.

Pike o' Blisco. From Langdale. From Wall End Farm by Kettle Ghyll with Ghyll well **R** to skyline, whence sharp **R** for summit. From Fell Foot incline **R** soon after crossing bridge a mile up pass.

Descents. Reverse routes or drop down to Red Tarn and **L** for Wrynose Gap.

Scafell Pike (*a*) from Esk Hause Shelter, facing Eskdale. Turn **R** towards Great End, which should certainly be climbed *en route.* On the top of steep bit beyond stream incline **L** and make for summit over ridges (rough, boulders).

(*b*) From Upper Eskdale. Walk up dale by **R** branch of Esk from Esk Falls to Cam Spout; cross stream, climb very steeply **L** to narrow Mickledore Ridge, which cross, and climb roughly direct to Pike (a very fagging course, especially towards finish).

(*c*) From Wasdale: **L,** through gate beyond school, cross bridge and turn immediately **R,** over a wall by an iron stile. Thence follow contour round the base of Lingmell, over another stile and wall, till the foot of Brown Tongue is reached after crossing a stream. From

Brown Tongue incline **L** to plateau between Lingmell and the Pike (Lingmell **L**, worth a visit). For Pike turn sharp **R** and follow cairns to summit (rough).

Descent. Reverse routes. The direction for Esk Hause (*see* above) is NE.

Scafell. Some half-mile from head of Wastwater, turn **R** through gate, cross two bridges, ascent **L** by Burnmoor track, midway between Screes and Scafell. At skyline **L** for summit. From Upper Eskdale follow Esk to just beyond Cam Spout, strike up sharp **L**, and again **L**, short of base of Mickledore Ridge, scrambling steeply and roughly to summit (not recommended), or preferably cross Burnmoor past Burnmoor Tarn till the Wasdale track is joined. Then **R** for summit. Return for Wasdale, Boot, or Upper Eskdale, due W., keeping Burnmoor Tarn well **L**. The route by the Tarn (852 ft.) is an easy ascent from Boot.

The Screes. From Wasdale. Follow Burnmoor track, turning **R** on reaching skyline.

Harter Fell, between Duddon Valley and Eskdale, is nearest Boot in Eskdale. It is also accessible from Coniston by Wrynose and Hardknott Passes. From head of Hardknott Pass, south for summit. Return, reverse routes, avoiding crags **L**.

(*f*) Great Gable Group (*see* p. 119)

Great and Green Gables, Kirkfell, Brandreth, Grey Knotts and Fleetwith Pike. Travelling moderate; rough towards Wasdale.

Great Gable (a very fine view-point). From Borrowdale *via* Honister Hause. Up fell by the former "drum-house" and over Grey Knotts, Brandreth, and Green Gable, to Wind Gap, whence ascend by cairns (nailmarks on rocks are a clearer guide), inclining generally **L** to avoid crags.

Descents. To Sty Head Tarn from Wind Gap (A). The usual route of ascent, but much inferior to the above.

To summit of Sty Head Pass (A). Face pony track to Esk Hause, steep. Avoid rocks to **R**.

To Gatesgarth *via* Scarth Gap. On north-west side of Great Gable cairns show the way down to depression between Gable and Kirk Fell. Hence down the valley northward, beside the stream, to the Youth Hostel opposite foot of Black Sail Pass, and near beginning of path through Scarth Gap.

To Gatesgarth from Grey Knotts. With back to Kirkfell, descend **L**, uninteresting, swampy, easy to get off track. Green Crag, at the head of Warnscale Bottom, must be kept well **L**, the descent being made on the Fleetwith side of the dale head.

Kirk Fell. From Black Sail Pass turn south and along wire fence as closely as crags will admit. Rough.

From Great Gable, cross intervening depression, keeping on Ennerdale side (rough).

Fleetwith Pike. From Honister Hause walk over the summit of

Honister Crag and descend steeply and roughly to Gatesgarth keeping the summit of the ridge (A).

(*g*) Newlands Group (*see* p. 100)

Dalehead, Hindscarth, Robinson. Travelling moderately easy, though precipices are numerous.

From Keswick. Row or walk to N. end of Catbells, follow ridge line over Maiden Moor and Eel Crags to above Rosthwaite, descend and turn **R** by Dalehead Tarn over Dalehead; with wire fence **L** and passing Hindscarth **R**, up Robinson, keeping rather to Buttermere side till the ascent **R** to the summit cairn. Thence the track runs **R** towards Newlands end of Hindscarth; it is easier going to turn rather more **R**. Follow the beck, with beck **R**, to Newlands church.

Descents. From depression N. of Dalehead Tarn facing Dalehead. **R** by track down Newlands Vale; **L** by trolley track direct to Rosthwaite, crossing the track to Grange along west side of the Derwent.

From beyond Dalehead over Hindscarth and down Scope End to Newlands (rough).

Between Hindscarth and Robinson, *via* Little Dale, following the *left* side of the stream to Newlands.

From Robinson by Buttermere Moss, keeping somewhat **L** at first to avoid crags, to Buttermere. From the Moss an old sledge-track leads out on to the Keswick road near Buttermere Hause. The general inclination after reaching Buttermere Moss is **R**.

The wire fence running from Dalehead to Robinson may be followed southwards to Honister Hause.

In misty weather keep a sharp look-out for quarries on the Yew Crag side of Dalehead. It is better to keep N. of the fence.

(*h*) High Raise Group (*see* p. 102)

Langdale Pikes, Sergeant Man, High Raise, Ullscarf. Travelling generally easy.

Langdale Pikes from Langdale—Dungeon Ghyll. (The Pikes themselves are ascended from behind—the north side.)

(1) With Ghyll **R** follow track **L** (roughish) to wet ground between Pikes till behind Pike 'o Stickle, passing beyond the head of the ghylls instead of crossing them.

(2) Ascend by Mill Gill, either side, to Stickle Tarn (1,540 feet), and climb **L** steeply between Pavey Ark and Harrison Stickle. Care must be taken in descending by this route to keep Harrison Stickle, the *highest* of the Pikes, **R**, and to keep midway between it and Pavey Ark (*see* p. 82).

(3) Sweep right round beyond tarn in a semi-circle, with tarn **L** the whole time, over Pavey Ark to Harrison Stickle and Pike o' Stickle, descending by Dungeon Ghyll, except in thick weather, when descend by Stake Pass, a long round.

From Grasmere by Blea Rigg. From Easedale Tarn, **L** to depression on Blea Rigg with crags **R.** Follow ridge **R** till Stickle Tarn is seen **L.** Ascend thence with Pavey Ark **L.** Steepish and swampy after Easedale Tarn. The views from the Pikes are fine, but inferior to those from—

High Raise, due north from Pikes over moorland (*see* p. 82), past Thunacar Knott, or by ridge line of Blea Rigg over Sergeant Man, with Manchester Corporation fence **R.** The ascent from Borrowdale is made from Greenup with Lining Crag **R,** after which incline **R.**

(*i*) Helvellyn Group (*see* p. 101)

Helvellyn and the Dodds, Raise, Fairfield, St. Sunday, Hart and Dove Crags, Dollywaggon Pike, and Red Screes. Travelling moderately easy. The distances are much greater than appears from the map—a rule in mountainous districts.

Helvellyn.—From Threlkeld there is a path **L** of quarries (avoid Wanthwaite Crags), or a more easy ascent a little way along the Matterdale track. All the Dodds and Raise are included, and from Helvellyn the walk may be continued by Grisedale Tarn or over Fairfield to Grasmere, or right on by Red Screes to Ambleside. By diversions **R** or **L** many of the minor points, which are too numerous to treat in detail, may be visited.

From Thirlspot. Incline **L,** and then with Fisher Ghyll **L,** turn **R** for summit along ridge line. Or, by wood beyond Thirlspot follow Helvellyn Ghyll, with Ghyll **L,** steeply to ridge line, which follow **R** over Low Man to summit.

From Wythburn. Pass church; turn **R** through gate up side of ravine, from top of which follow track **L** for summit.

From Glenridding turn **R** to Greenside Smelting Mill, then go *straight on* (the track **R** joins Sticks Pass) towards the dry bed of Keppelcove Tarn, then ascend **R** with tarn **L,** sweeping round the heights above the tarn for summit **L.**

By Swirrel Edge. Passing Greenside Mill follow **L** branch of stream and by white posts to Red Tarn, and with tarn **L** climb ridge and scramble thence to summit (rough, steep, boulders). [Track to Edge not given on map. It is longer but preferable to take the Striding Edge route (*see* below) as far as the gate in the wall.]

By Striding Edge. Turn up Grisedale (midway between Patterdale and Glenridding), then **R** by signpost by copse and **L** by zigzag path to gate in wall, and along Edge (with tarn **R**). The final climb is trying—special care must be taken descending.* (Between two last routes a track **L** from Glenridding leads over Birkhouse Moor to this gate.) Neither Edge recommended for the inexperienced.

From Patterdale or Grasmere by Grisedale Tarn. Strike path

*** When descending, particularly in bad visibility, it is well to remember that "walk-off" for Striding Edge is some 50 yards below the Gough memorial.**

steeply up Dollywaggon Pike, which visit, and thence by ridge line to summit. This is the continuation of the route over—

Fairfield from Ambleside. By Sweden Bridge (p. 62) and Scandale to skyline. Then to Dove Crag, thence **L** round head of Rydal by Hart Crag (rough) to summit.

Descents (facing Red Screes) by Dove Crag to Scandale Head and **R** to Ambleside or **L** by Caiston Glen to Kirkstone Foot.

For Patterdale, incline (back to Red Screes) **R** at first, by narrow ridge (Cofa Pike) to St. Sunday Crag, thence down **L** to Grisedale from the first depression beyond St. Sunday Crag.

For Grisedale Pass follow stone wall west to head of pass by tarn.

For Grasmere or Rydal (facing Grasmere). Go straight ahead over Great Rigg; path divides—(*a*) Along **R** ridge line for Grasmere (the easiest way, between Stone Arthur and Greenhead Ghyll), pony track; (*b*) along **L** ridge line to Heron Pike; path again divides; (*c*) **R** for Grasmere or (*d*) straight on for Rydal somewhat roughly over Nab Scar and steeply thence to Rydal, inclining **L.** These all are excellent lines of ascent.

Red Screes from Ambleside. About a mile up Kirkstone Pass turn **L** and follow up ridge line over Snarker Pike for summit, whence descend, inclining **L** to wall at Scandale Head. Red Screes may also be reached by following the Sweden Bridge route (*see* Fairfield, above) and turning **R** instead of **L** as for Dove Crag. This is the least arduous ascent.

From Patterdale by Kirkstone Pass, turning **R** beyond Brothers' Water, and by Caiston Glen to Scandale Head and then **L** to summit.

Place Fell from Patterdale. Take road almost opposite **Post** Office, then **R** by path to Boardale Hause; then **L** to summit.

Descents. For Howtown continue inclining **R** to Boardale and so by Cowgarth or follow ridge line to first depression, whence by grass path turn **L** and then **R** for lake side (somewhat rough).

(*k*) High Street Group (*see* p. 111)*

High Street, Kidsty Pike, Ill Bell, Froswick, Caudale Moor, Harter Fell, High Raise, etc. Travelling generally easy. Some fine lofty crags. This group is even more suitable than the foregoing for a "watershed walk," with excursions **R** and **L.** Best undertaken from north to south.

Steamer from Pooley Bridge to Howtown, whence follow Fusedale Beck up to its fork; then **L** to **Weather Hill,** or **R** from Howtown to Cowgarth, thence **L** past wood, **R** by long ridge line to midway between Weather Hill and High Raise.

With Ullswater **L** visit **Loadpot Hill.** The Roman Road may be followed thence **L** to near **Tirril.** There is a road **R** to Askham and Lowther Castle.

* The dales west of High Street are largely deer forest. Descents towards Haweswater bring one down to the path on the western shore: the Haweswater Hotel is on the eastern shore.

For ascents *from Gatescarthfoot, see* p. 111.

Descents. From Roman Road with Ullswater **R.**

From Weather Hill to Haweswater. Descend **L;** from Low Kop incline **R** to Measand Beck; cross at foot-bridge.

After passing **High Raise,** from **Kidsty Pike** (somewhat rough), **L** by track down broken shoulder between becks for Riggindale and Haweswater, inclining **R** on lower slopes (steep). **R** with Haweswater, inclining **R** on lower slopes (steep). **R** with Hayeswater **L,** for Hayeswater Ghyll. Cross, and with ghyll **R** go to Low Hartsop, continuing for Patterdale. The **R** branch of this track from above Hayeswater is a ridge-line walk by Angle Tarn to Boardale Hause.

From **High Street (L),** roughly and narrowly, by Rough Crag **(L)** to Mardale, inclining **L** on lower slopes.

From High Street incline **L** round Blea Water and continue on ridge to head of Nan Bield Pass, whence path descends by Small Water to Gatescarthfoot.

Following Roman Road to **Thornthwaite Crag** (in misty weather follow wall to cairn on Thornthwaite Crag), whence are many routes.

From Thornthwaite Crag (a fine view-point), facing Windermere, steeply **R** to **Thresthwaite Mouth** and **R** by Pasture Beck to Brothers' Water. (From the Hause a rough ascent conducts over Caudale Moor to Kirkstone Pass, inclining **L.)**

From Thornthwaite Crag (by Roman Road) or **Thresthwaite** Hause you can reach Troutbeck for Windermere.

Best to continue S. by **Froswick** and **Ill Bell** over **Yoke** to Garburn Pass for Windermere.

Harter Fell, between Nan Bield Pass and Gatescarth Pass, which divides it from Branstree. The best line is from the head of one pass to the head of the other, keeping on the top of the slope which descends towards Mardale. Avoid bearing south. The faces towards Haweswater are steep.

(*l*) Coniston Group (*See* p. 84)

Old Man, Carrs, Wetherlam, Great How Crags, Swirl How, Dow Crags, Grey Friar. Travelling generally easy, but there is much rough ground, and quarries are a danger.

Ascents to the Old Man (*see* p. 84).

From Church follow Church Beck **R** or **L** to near bridge; then through gate on south bank and **R** by stiles over walls and skirting a slope (a road from Walna Scar route joins this route), then uphill for Low Water, with quarrymen's huts **R.** There are numerous and misleading miners' paths here. With tarn **R** steeply to summit, inclining **L** first and **R** at end.

From Walna Scar Pass **R** up the shoulder from beyond Boo Tarn (A).

From farther along the pass westwards, **R,** by Goats Water from foot of tarn.

From the head of pass **R** over **Dow Crags** (precipitous), thence ncline **R** round Gaits (Goat's) Water to **Old Man**.

From Old Man with Low Water **R** go N. to **Brim Fell.** Thence to Swirl How. Incline **L,** with Seathwaite Tarn **L,** and visit **Grey Friars,** thence sharply **R** to **Carrs.** Thence continue N., inclining **R** at first and then **L** direct to the head of Wrynose (rough).

From Swirl How, between Carrs and Great How Crags, there is a steep descent in an easterly direction (keeping on the Coniston side), followed by ascent to the summit of Wetherlam, *the second, not the first, elevation.*

Descents from Wetherlam, facing Langdale.

To Little Langdale. Incline **R** along ridge line, and then **L,** making for some copper works. Unpleasant.

To Tilberthwaite, as above, curving round **R** from ridge line. Tiresome.

For Coniston, with back to Langdale, follow the ridge line to a well-marked depression whence a path leads down **R** to near copper mines.

Motoring in the Lake District

The District is too constricted in area and in the number of its roads to form a touring ground in the sense usually understood by the 200-mile-a-day motorist. Those who proceed to visit the various dales from a single centre, however, will quickly appreciate the utility, not to say necessity, of a car, since the intercepting fells are in very few cases crossed by roads, and dale villages only 3 miles distant in a direct line may be separated by a dozen miles of road, or even more. A car is often a boon, too, at the beginning or end of a long day's walking. (Climbers will rarely have difficulty in finding farms or hotels where the car may be parked for a few hours.) Moreover, although the District is small—say 25 miles each way—a ride of only a few miles will take one to the other side of a group of fells, present them in a new beauty of outline or colour, and generally give at least as great a sense of change as many a 100-mile run in flatter country.

With a few exceptions the roads are notably safe for so mountainous a district—the average motorist will find greater anxieties in the numerous heavy motor-coaches. On some of the secondary roads it is necessary to proceed with caution on account of the curves, many of them "blind"; places where oncoming traffic can prove trying at times, to say the least. Another feature of the by-roads are the gates, which are generally kept closed to prevent sheep from straying, and which form a real danger to the unwary motorist.

For Road Routes to the District *see* p. 9.

The Roads of the Lake District

Inasmuch as a large proportion of the visitors to the District travel by car or coach over its delightful roads, we have thought it well to say something of the scenery which contributes so abundantly to the enjoyment of such drives. Space will not permit of detailed reference to all the roads.

The by-roads are therefore omitted altogether and some of the approach roads are only described when they come within the limits of the Lake District proper. Fuller descriptions of many scenes will be found with the aid of the Index at the end of the book.

We open with the great Trunk Road:

WINDERMERE (BOWNESS) TO KESWICK (22 miles)

Route.—Road good throughout, with no dangerous gradients. Being the principal thoroughfare in the District, however, it is apt to be very crowded in the season. The slightly longer route by the *western* shore of Thirlmere is less busy.

From the landing at Bowness, keeping to the left beyond the Royal Hotel. The houses are soon left behind and there are fine views across the waters of Windermere. First the fine bluff of Wetherlam is seen and a little later a glorious panorama, extending from the Coniston Fells to the Langdale Pikes, opens. The conspicuous peak is Bowfell, on the left of which a glimpse of the summit of Scafell Pike may be obtained. The square-headed fell on its right is Great Gable. About a mile from Bowness, Millerground landing and bathing place is passed, and shortly beyond it the main Windermere-Keswick road is joined. Here bear left. For some way views of the Lake are hidden by walls and trees, but there are occasional glances through inviting vistas, and at Low Wood Hotel an even more beautiful panorama comes into view, the Langdale Pikes looking their best. Before long these disappear behind Loughrigg, which gradually blocks the scenery in that direction. **Waterhead** is the northern terminus of the Windermere boat services, and the "port" of **Ambleside.**

In the centre of Ambleside we bear down to the left, soon passing the Old Bridge House. For the next few miles the road narrows and winds considerably. Pelter Bridge makes a pretty scene, and then the road winds through the hamlet of Rydal and there is revealed sweet **Rydal Water.** The road runs within a few yards of the lake for almost its entire length. About midway a miniature by-pass indicates the efforts made to preserve Nab Cottage (*see* p. 63); then the road curves round the head of Rydal and through woods beyond which **Grasmere Lake** appears very beautifully. The mountain at the far end, to the left of Grasmere village, is Silver How, and a little farther on a white streak in a recess on the left shows where Sour Milk Gill descends from Easedale Tarn. On the right, a short distance beyond the *Prince of Wales Hotel* is the lane leading to Wordsworth's Cottage; on the left is the road to **Grasmere** village, but the Keswick road keeps straight ahead and soon begins the long steady ascent of **Dunmail Raise.** The backward views are increasingly interesting as the road rises, but ahead the most striking feature is the detached mass of Helm Crag, to the left of the road. On the right Stone Arthur stands up well, and beyond the Grisedale Pass opens up, with Seat Sandal on its left, but the slopes of the Helvellyn range are too close to be appreciated. The spur which descends from the left to Dunmail Raise is Steel Fell. Descending the northern side of Dunmail Raise we soon get a pretty glimpse of Thirlmere, with the very steep flanks of Helvellyn on the right. **Thirlmere** itself is so masked by trees as to be rather hidden from the roads bordering it. At the foot of the Raise the road along the western side of Thirlmere goes off on the left—it is narrower and more winding than the main road, but is prettier, although the views of Helvellyn's mighty flank do not compare with the mountain views from the main road. The two roads rejoin near the northern end of the Lake. A short way beyond the foot of the Raise is **Wythburn** hamlet, with its white-walled church. Some three miles farther on the trees which have screened the Lake give way and there are good views not only of Thirlmere but of the wooded Raven Crag on the far side. The Lake disappears from view again as we run in behind Great Howe. Half a mile farther we bear left to Smeathwaite Bridge, and soon begin the ascent which suddenly reveals **Keswick** and the superbly-set **Derwentwater.** To the right is Bassenthwaite, with Skiddaw seen almost from head to foot on its right. Then the "delighted eye" travels round over the Lorton Fells, the graceful cone of Grisedale Pike and the rounded bulk of Grassmoor right to the Scafell range: a lovely ring of graceful heights in front of which Derwentwater gleams in the sun.

ROUND WINDERMERE LAKE (27 miles)

Motorists may be advised to regard the very fine road between Newby Bridge and Windermere as some compensation for the rough—if more beautiful—roads on the western side of the Lake. Those for whom bad roads have no allure may make a round trip over good roads by way of Newby Bridge—Graythwaite, the western side of Esthwaite Water and Hawkshead—Clappersgate–Ambleside—Windermere.

BORROWDALE AND BUTTERMERE BY THE HONISTER ROAD

The building of the road over Honister, between Buttermere and Borrowdale, has made a circular run *via* Buttermere perfectly safe and open to all careful motorists, a fact which is difficult to realise in view of the long-standing notoriety of the old Honister road, with its deadly surface.

Those who do not desire so long a round can be recommended to return from Rosthwaite by the Keswick road as far as Grange, where cross the bridge and bear to the right, returning to Keswick by the western shore of Derwentwater: a very lovely run, especially at evening.

Windermere, from Orrest Head (*Valentine*)

Waterhead, Ambleside (*Valentine*)

Rydal Water (*J. Hardman*)

Grasmere and Rydal Water (*T. Parker*)

From Keswick the road runs along the eastern side of the Lake. On the left come first the wooded hummock of Castle Head, then Walla Crag, cleft by the great rift of the Lady's Rake, then Falcon Crag, and so by Barrow Woods. The glory of the scenery is on the right, **Derwentwater** in all its loveliness with Catbells rising along the farther side and the noble background of the Grassmoor Fells beyond. Then, over the dip to Buttermere Hause appear the Buttermere Fells, with Robinson on the left and the summit of Hindscarth seen over Catbells. These are soon shut off by Catbells, except the perky tip of Causey Pike. At the southern end of the Lake is the double bridge at Grange, beyond which we are fairly within the jaws of **Borrowdale,** and the Fells close in. On the left is Grange Fell; on the opposite side are Maiden Moor and Scawdell Fell. The prominent buttress a short distance above Grange is Gate Crag, and, immediately beyond, Castle Crag divides the dale. The handsome mountain which seems to close the dale-head is Glaramara. Road and river run in company between rocks and trees to the beautiful open strath of **Rosthwaite.** Shortly before reaching the village, the rounded front of Lingmell and the sharper peak of Gable may be seen. Beyond Rosthwaite a fine valley opens on the left with Eagle Crag standing proudly at the foot of Langstrath. Thanks to the building of the road over Honister, it is no longer necessary for motorists to turn back at **Seatoller.** Instead, they may turn up by the road which follows more or less the route of the original Honister road (*i.e.* before the building of the toll-road) and climb steadily if steeply to **Honister Hause,** whence, as the quarry buildings are passed, there is a very striking view down towards Buttermere (*see* p. 95). From Buttermere to Keswick there is either the hilly road *via* Newlands Pass (turn up to right by Buttermere church) or that by Crummock Water and Whinlatter Pass (*see* p. 50). For **Seathwaite** turn left about 200 yards short of Seatoller. This is a cul-de-sac.

WASDALE

Route.—Wasdale can be entered or left only from the west, and to reach it from, say, Ambleside or Keswick one must ride half-way round the District—but, it is worth it. From Keswick to Scalehill, Loweswater, Ennerdale Bridge and Calder Bridge, or *via* Bassenthwaite and Cockermouth; from Ambleside *via* Coniston and Broughton; from Windermere *via* Newby Bridge, Greenodd and Broughton.

After the mountainous glories of real Lakeland roads the run through the flatter country between the fells and the sea offers a fair contrast and has the effect of whetting one's appetite to appreciate still more keenly the wild beauty of Wasdale. After passing Strands and entering the woods, the tremendous buttress of the Screes may be seen through openings in the foliage. Then we come to the deep, challenging beauty of Wastwater itself, with the strange rampart of the Screes, half forbidding, half alluring, overlooking it. On the left we pass Buckbarrow, Middlefell, and Bowderdale, with occasional peeps of Red Pike and parts of Scoatfell, turning at length below the rugged cone of Yewbarrow. The head of the dale is impressive in the extreme. Right in front is the cloven face of Pikes Crag on Scafell Pike. On its right just a fringe of the great Scafell precipice may be seen. On its left are Lingmell, the Styhead Pass, the striking pyramid of Great Gable, and Kirkfell falling steeply to gloomy Mosedale and the Black Sail Pass.

CRUMMOCK WATER AND BUTTERMERE

Route.—From Keswick by Honister or the Whinlatter Pass.

What has been said concerning the setting of Wastwater is approximately true of Crummock. The fells at the foot of the Lake are graceful yet lack distinction, gaining in character in Melbreak, which flanks the western shore. On the left Whiteside and Grassmoor descend with striking steepness almost to the water's edge. In front the Buttermere Red Pike lifts its shapely head. Passing the rocky projection of Rannerdale Knotts we soon come on Buttermere. Across the Lake are Red Pike, High Stile and High Crag, and, beyond, Warnscale Bottom, buttressed by Haystacks on the right and Fleetwith Pike on the left. A walk of a few steps up Buttermere Hause brings Great Gable into sight. By following the road below Robinson past Hassness to Gatesgarth one reaches the foot of **Honister Pass,** the scene of so many struggles between car and contour in the past, but now equipped with a well-made modern road which reduces the toil and danger to a minimum though the gradients are still severe.

The road ends at Seatoller, where we rejoin the Keswick road described in an earlier route.

As an alternative return from Buttermere the road climbing steeply beside the church can be recommended to those who do not mind hills and narrow lanes. It regains Keswick by way of Newlands Pass, otherwise Buttermere Hause.

WINDERMERE TO PATTERDALE AND PENRITH

The ascent from or descent to Ambleside is extremely steep. The more reasonable course is by way of Troutbeck. It is all uphill till the summit of the Pass is reached; thence to Brothers' Water it is a long, steep, winding descent.

From Bowness Pier take the road past Millerground to Cooks House on the Windermere–Ambleside road, and then keep straight ahead past Troutbeck Church up the rising road which climbs the side of the steep valley containing the Trout Beck. The road rounds Wansfell and in approaching the Inn on **Kirkstone Pass** gives a fine view of the head of Windermere, with Stockgill and the precipitous hill coming up from Ambleside.

The summit of the Pass is 1,476 feet above the sea. A little beyond the Inn and on the left is the Kirk Stone, more easily recognisable from the Patterdale side. Care is required, as the road descends very steeply. On the right is Caudale Moor, on the left Red Screes. In front is Place Fell. After a while the Caiston Glen comes down on the left and immediately afterwards we pass **Brothers' Water.** The yellow house on the far side is Hartsop Hall, for three centuries the property of the Lowthers, but acquired for the nation in 1946. Behind on the left come in quick succession Dovedale with Dove Crag standing up grandly at its head and then Deepdale backed by the grim precipice of Fairfield. Next we pass through **Patterdale** (17 m.) and so to **Glenridding.** In the neighbourhood of Patterdale Church a glimpse of Striding Edge may be caught high up on the left. Patterdale is at the southern end of Ullswater; at the northern end is Pooley Bridge, and the road connecting them keeps close to the western shore all the way. It is a pretty run, but the best views are over one's shoulder. Beyond Pooley Bridge the scenery is definitely pastoral all the way to **Penrith** (26½ m.). Half a mile short of Pooley Bridge there is an alternative road by Dalemain.

CONISTON TO AMBLESIDE (8 miles)

Routes.—There are two routes; of which that described below is the more picturesque. The other route, *via* Barn Gates, may well be used for the return.

By Oxenfell. From the church take the road past the *Black Bull Hotel* up **Yewdale.** After about half a mile the buttress of Yewdale Crag stands out on the left; a mile farther the valley of Tilberthwaite opens on the same side, with Raven Crag at its mouth. Our road runs to the right, along below Holme Fell. The artificial lakelet is Yew Tree Tarn. On the right is the long range of low heights which extends round about Tarn Hows. The scenery here is perhaps a little tame, especially when compared with the glorious surprise view which greets one from Colwith Brow. A slight leftward turn of the head takes in Wetherlam and then come the Crinkle Crags, Bowfell, Pike o' Blisco, and then the Langdale Pikes, with the Langdales and Elterwater in beauty at their feet. In front from north to south extends an unbroken line of fells from Helvellyn through the Fairfield range, with Red Screes prominent, to Ill Bell. A steep descent leads to **Skelwith Bridge,** and then runs more or less by the riverside to **Ambleside.**

AMBLESIDE TO DUNGEON GHYLL

The road from Ambleside is by Rothay Bridge and Clappersgate and thence follows the northern bank of the Brathay to Skelwith Bridge. The road winds round the foot of Loughrigg and shortly Elterwater appears on the left. Keep straight ahead at the crossroads and through Chapel Stile village. Then in front is seen one of the finest mountain groupings in the Lakes. High up on the right is the precipice of Pavey Ark. In front is Harrison Stickle and next to it Loft Crag, with the sheer face of Gimmer Crag below (Pike o' Stickle cannot be seen). On the far side of the vale is the "many-fountained" Pike o' Blisco, leading on to the wild Crinkles and the imposing peak of Bowfell.

The road into the heart of Great Langdale cannot now be mistaken. **Dungeon Ghyll,** a fine ravine, can be reached from either the *New* or the *Old* Hotel. Beyond the *Old Hotel,* where the buses stop, the road turns sharply to the left and then makes for the farm of Wall End, at the foot of Pike o' Blisco. Continuing on, a fair road winds past Bleatarn House with Blea Tarn on our right and, in another mile Little Langdale Tarn. A mile farther west are Colwith Bridge and Force and thence it is convenient to join the Coniston road, turning left at the top of the steep brow, and descend to Skelwith Bridge where the Ambleside road is obvious.

The Southern (Windermere) Section

The chief centres in this section are grouped round Windermere, viz., Bowness and the town of Windermere (practically one), on its eastern side; Ambleside and Grasmere, near its northern end; and Coniston, some five miles westward of Windermere (eleven by road).

We shall describe each in turn, with the principal walks and road trips therefrom, premising that, as the first three centres are so near and so closely linked by road and boat services, the excursions are almost interchangeable, and can in many cases be taken almost as conveniently from one centre as from another. This is especially true as regards the motor trips.

BOWNESS AND WINDERMERE

Approach.—For Road Routes *See* p. 9.

Rail.—London Midland Region *via* Oxenholme. Through carriages are run from Manchester and London. *See also* p. 8.

Banks.—*Barclays; District; Midland.*

Bathing.—Near Millerground landing.

Boats (Bowness and Millerground).—All types of boats available for hire.

Bowls.—Queen's Park and Longlands.

Buses.—Constant service of buses between Windermere, Waterhead, Ambleside, Grasmere, Newby Bridge, Kendal and Keswick. There is a regular service of buses between Windermere station and the pier at Bowness.

Car Parking.—*Bowness:* Rectory Road, adjoining Promenade, Church Street, Lake Road, and Glebe Road; Braithwaite Fold. *Windermere:* Broad Street.

Cinema at Bowness.

Coaches to Grasmere, Keswick, Patterdale, Furness Abbey and many places farther afield.

Early Closing.—Thursday.

Ferry.—Between Ferry Nab, about a mile below Bowness, and the Ferry House on the western shore, a ferry plies regularly carrying motor cycles and cars.

Golf.—18-hole course on the Kendal Road, about a mile from Bowness Pier. *See* p. 18. Miniature golf and putting in the Glebe, adjoining Promenade.

Hotels.—Bowness *Belsfield; Burnside; Windermere Hydro; Cranleigh; Old England; Royal; Stag's Head; Storrs Hall,* 2 m. south. Windermere: *Windermere; Elleray; Langdale Chase; Low Wood,* 3 m. on Ambleside road; *Applegarth; Wild Boar,* 3 m. on Crook road; *Sun,* Troutbeck Bridge, 1 mile; and many others.

Lake Side: *Lake Side.*

Library, with reading-rooms, etc., at Ellerthwaite.

Motor Boats.—H.Q. of Windermere Motor Boat Club are at Broad Leys and races are held every Saturday during the season.

Places of Worship.—*Parish Church* (Bowness), *St. Mary's, St. John's, St. Herbert's Roman Catholic, Congregational, Methodist* and *Plymouth Brethren.*

Population.—7,680.

Post Office.—Head Office, Crescent Road, Windermere; and branch offices,

Ash Street, Bowness, Park Road, Heathwaite, and at Troutbeck Bridge.
Public Hall.—Lake Road.
Putting Green.—Near the Promenade.
Railway Station in Windermere.
Reading Room and Library, Ellerthwaite.
Steamer Pier at Bowness.
Tennis.—The Promenade, Bowness.
Yachting.—The headquarters of the Royal Windermere Yacht Club are on Bowness Bay; *South Windermere Sailing Club* at Fellfoot.

Windermere and Bowness are two villages which together form a small town. They are on the eastern side of the Lake, about four miles from its head, Windermere inland, Bowness on the water's edge.

Owing to its natural beauty, protected situation, and other attractive features, the place is popular not only as a holiday resort but as a permanent summer and winter residence. Much of it is modern and there are many attractive houses embowered in trees and shrubs and surrounded by beautiful gardens. Windermere station is nearly five hundred feet above sea-level, and fully three hundred feet above the Lake, from which it is distant by the road to Bowness nearly a mile and three-quarters, though the shore at Millerground is within three-quarters of a mile, half an hour's easy walk.

St. Mary's Church, a few hundred yards on the Ambleside road, was dedicated in 1856. It has a chiming clock. Not far from the station, a little north of the road, is the old cottage at **Elleray,** once the residence of Professor Wilson.

At the junction of the roads from Windermere station to Bowness is a **Clock-Tower** built by subscriptions in 1907 to the memory of the late M. J. B. Baddeley, whose famous Guide to the Lake District is now issued, with revisions, from the same office as this volume.

Bowness

has been well described as a "labyrinth of small streets" in which it is equally difficult for a stranger to lose his way or to decide off-hand exactly where he is, though now the main road is well defined. It contains numerous pretty residences and boarding-houses, and is a good centre for boating and other excursions. The **Church** is an ancient structure, with square tower, dedicated to St. Martin—of whom it contains an ancient wooden carving. A few moments at least should be spared to examine the beautiful east window one of the oldest in the kingdom, taken from Cartmel Priory (*see* p. 134). The three lights in the centre, representing the Crucifixion, form one of the finest examples of glass painting extant. Of considerably greater interest to trans-Atlantic visitors is the pane near the top of the third light from the right, for it displays the arms of John Washington (1403), twelfth ancestor of George Washington. With the aid of field-glasses one can examine the Washington coat of arms, with the stars and stripes.

It may be noted that this Church near the Lake is the Parish Church of Windermere, a parish which includes the bottom and therefore all the islands in the Lake, and such an incongruity as Lake Side Station, built on piles near the foot of the Lake, some six miles away.

Bowness—which, by the way, should be pronounced Bōwness, not Bownéss—is the real "port" of the Lake and the centre for fishing. Yachting and boating are popular activities, and the races and other competitions excite keen interest. At Bowness Bay are the headquarters of the well-known Royal Windermere Yacht Club.

On a knoll near the Pier is a bandstand, and close at hand are beautifully situated tennis courts, and putting greens and **Car Parks**. Southward is an excellent **Miniature Golf Course.**

WINDERMERE

Steamers and Boats.—Motor vessels of British Railways Shipping Division operate a frequent service between Lake Side, Bowness and Waterhead, Ambleside.

There are also numerous motor-boat excursions from various piers.

Windermere has a length from north to south of about ten miles, with a maximum width of a mile.

From **Lake Side,** at the southern end of the Lake, the comfortable motor vessels of British Railways start on their trips up this fine sheet of water, the largest in England. Though the lower reaches are tamer than the upper ones, the trip is very enjoyable. The hill on the east side of the lake nearly opposite the Lake Side Hotel is **Gummer's How**

(1,054 ft.). In the woods behind the hotel there are paths leading to **Finsthwaite Tower,** erected "to honour the officers, seamen, and marines of the Royal Navy, whose matchless conduct and irresistible valour decisively defeated the fleets of France, Spain, and Holland, and promoted and protected liberty and commerce, 1799."

Newby Bridge (*Swan, Newby Bridge*) is situated amid pretty surroundings on the Leven, a mile from the foot of the lake. The name is derived from the quaint old-world bridge, with five low arches of unequal sizes and sharply-pointed buttresses. The recesses in which walkers may take refuge when endangered by passing motoring maniacs are as necessary now as when first built. Many anglers find the spot to their liking.

A mile farther is **Backbarrow,** a village on the Leven, and the home of two old, established cottage industries, "swilling" and oak spale basket making. There is also a blue works. The Leven here tumbles over three pretty falls, the largest in the district as regards volume.

Lake Side to Waterhead

On the northern horizon is a grand array of fells from **Fairfield** to **Ill Bell,** and **Helvellyn** comes into sight almost immediately after we leave the pier. Proceeding up the Lake we pass, in rather more than a mile, **Blake Holme,** on the eastern shore, with the promontory of **Long Tongue** jutting from the opposite side. **Silver Holme** guards the little bay formed by the Tongue. **Grass Holme** next comes into sight; then **Rawlinson Nab,** with Cunsey House and Cunsey Wood behind it; next **Ling Holme,** at the mouth of *Cunsey Beck.* In this stretch we get glimpses of the Langdale Pikes, the Coniston Fells, and Bowfell with a peep of Scafell Pike. These are all on the west side of Windermere. The next object of interest, on the opposite shore, is *Storrs Hall*, now an hotel. The hall will always be associated with the visit of the "giants" of literature to its then owner, Mr. Bolton, as recorded in Lockhart's *Life of Scott*.

Ramp Holme is next passed, and, almost immediately

afterwards the beautifully situated Ferry House. A ferry takes the road traffic from Kendal to Hawkshead across the lake between Ferry House and the Ferry Nab opposite.

From this point the mountain view keeps rising until we are a little south of Low Wood, when to the east and immediately ahead it begins to deteriorate. To the right the cone-shaped peak is Ill Bell, with the High Street range and Caudale Moor to the left (west). Then comes the massive form of Red Screes, which continues the mountain outline over Dove Crag, Hart Crag to Fairfield and Great Rigg. The low, richly-coloured Loughrigg fills in the foreground. Next in order, turning westwards, are the graceful Langdale Pikes and the noble peak of Bowfell, the interspace being filled by Allen Crags, with Great Gable beyond. On the other side of Bowfell one catches sight of Scafell Pike again. Then the wild Crinkle Crags descend to Wrynose, overlooking which is the bold outline of Wetherlam, the easternmost height of the Coniston range, which culminates in the Old Man, conspicuous by its cairn.

Leaving the Ferry. we see right before us the largest of the islands on Windermere—indeed, the only one of any size—**Curwen Island,** or **Belle Isle** (named after the Curwens, descendants in direct line from Ivo de Taillebois, who came over with the Conqueror). This island is owned by the Lake District Planning Board; most of the other islands may be explored at will.

Sailing along the eastern side of the island, we call at **Bowness** pier. Continuing our course to the head of the Lake, the surroundings become grander. Among the many islets **St. Mary's,** or **Lady Holme** attracts attention. The name is derived from a chantry dedicated to the Virgin Mary, which was standing in the reign of Henry VIII, but of which no traces remain. It was given to the National Trust in 1937.

The vessel glides by the fine woods of **Rayrigg** and **Elleray.** Rayrigg Hall, standing near the water's edge, was for several years the summer residence of William Wilberforce. **Queen Adelaide's Hill,** farther along the bank, is now National Trust property, as is also the boat-landing of **Millerground,** where there is bathing and boating. We next pass the woods of Calgarth Hall. formerly the residence of Bishop Watson of

Llandaff. On the western shore is **High Wray.** Along the western shore, as far as High Wray, a range of rocky fells rises over the water, covered here and there with birch, oak, hazel and pine, bracken and heather. At about this point Wansfell Pike intervenes and shuts out Ill Bell and the High Street range. The Langdale and Coniston fells, however, are now seen in all their glory. On the Lancashire shore is **Wray Castle** (now only a shell). The grounds, however, are open to the public. Not long after we leave Low Wood, the Langdale Pikes disappear behind Loughrigg.

We now rapidly approach the head of Windermere, passing Dove Nest, for one summer the residence of Mrs. Hemans, and Wansfell Holme. Towards the north, surrounding the head of the Lake, are the lofty mountains beyond Ambleside, "the stern and bleak companions of the mist and cloud."

The chief rivers into Windermere are the *Trout Beck*, the *Brathay* and the *Rothay.* The last two unite near Croft Lodge and flow into the head of the Lake. The Brathay rises at the foot of the Wrynose Pass and is the boundary between Lancashire and Westmorland. The Rothay rises above Dunmail Raise, and links the lakes of Grasmere and Rydal.

WALKS NEAR WINDERMERE AND BOWNESS

Numerous delightful strolls may be taken in the neighbourhood, not the least pleasing being by the footpaths that run from Windermere village through the woods to the lake side.

1. **Orrest Head,** immediately to the north of Windermere village, is a spot which no one should omit to visit. The prospect is of exquisite beauty, from Windermere Lake, which is seen in its entire length, and its soft surroundings, to the rugged fells that wall in the head of Langdale. All the mountains seen from the steamer (pp. 56–8) are visible, and in addition a massive portion of the Scafell range comes into view between Bowfell and Crinkle Crags.

Other short walks affording charming views of lake, woodland and mountain are:

2. To Biskey Howe and Post Knott descending straight to the Kendal road at Burnside.

3. To Biskey Howe, Matson Ground, and the Golf Course.
4. To School Knott, by Lickbarrow or Droomer.
5. Along the road parallel with the Lake, passing Rayrigg Hall, to Adelaide Hill and Miller Brow.
6. Past "Christopher North's" Cottage through the **Elleray** woods to the Troutbeck road.
7. To the **Ferry,** by the Public Park and Cockshot Point; by the Ferry to Ferry House.
8. A longer walk is to **Newby Bridge** and **Lake Side,** 9 miles, by Winster and Bowland Bridge. On this walk a visit should be paid to **Cartmel Fell Church.** Notice especially the east window, which was probably originally in Cartmel Priory, as was that of Bowness Church (*see* p. 134). From Lake Side one may return on foot along the western side of Windermere; for most of the way the road itself is more beautiful than the much-modernised road along the eastern shore, but the views from it are more in the nature of glimpses through the trees. Most people, however, prefer to take steamer from Lake Side to Bowness.

9. To **Ambleside.** (Walk or by bus). From Windermere by the main road from the station; from Bowness by the turning by the Royal Hotel. The roads unite at Cook's House. The road passes the industrial village of Troutbeck Bridge and is out of sight of the lake as far as Ecclerigg. The lake-side is reached again at Low Wood, from which the outlook is very fine, the Langdale Pikes and Bowfell being conspicuous.

From Ambleside we may return along the western side of the Lake by Clappersgate, Brathay Bridge, High Wray, and the Ferry. As a return route it is hardly to be recommended, as one has one's back to the best of the scenery, but it is a very pleasant way of reaching Ambleside. Total round about twelve miles.

10. To **Kirkstone Pass** by Troutbeck, returning by Ambleside. (Walk or Drive. If driving, the return journey should be made by Troutbeck as the direct descent to Ambleside is very steep.) The Troutbeck road turns to the right out of the Ambleside road a little over half a mile from Windermere at Cook's House cross-roads.

About three miles after leaving the Ambleside road we reach the church of **Troutbeck,** which has some good stained glass by Burne Jones and others in the east window. The village (*Mortal Man, Queen's Head, Glenside, Birkhead*) is a straggling line of cottages and farmsteads, clustered on the western slope of the valley.

Troutbeck was famous in olden times for its "statesmen" (among them an uncle of Hogarth, the painter); its wrestlers, men of great strength; the longevity of its inhabitants; its superstitions (mostly of Scandinavian origin); and its renowned *Mortal Man Inn.* The old building is not recognisable in the modern hotel. Note Inn Sign.

Some four miles more uphill leads to the **Kirkstone Pass** (*see* p. 78). A steep descent of three miles brings us to Ambleside, whence a return is made to Bowness by the main road. The total round is about fourteen miles, of which the last four can be saved by taking the bus or steamer from Waterhead to Bowness.

Variation (walk). Rather more than half a mile short of the Kirkstone Pass there is a path to the left leading to the Grove Farm and on to Ambleside by **Stock Ghyll Force.** This way is rather shorter and pleasanter than the other.

If the reverse route be selected, it is as well to take boat or bus from Bowness to Ambleside, returning by Troutbeck.

11. The **Troutbeck Valley.** This beautiful valley extends for about eight miles in a southerly direction from the foot of High Street to Calgarth Park and Windermere, and affords a charming and easy ramble.

Proceed as in Walk 10 as far as Troutbeck village. From this point various tracks lead towards the head of the valley, that to the right of Troutbeck Tongue being, if anything, the pleasantest.

Westward the valley is bounded by **Wansfell** (1,597 ft.), and to the north-east by a semi-circle of lofty mountains, **Yoke** (south of Ill Bell), the twin peaks of **Ill Bell** (2,476 ft.), and **Froswick,** the Thornthwaite Crag end of **High Street** (here 2,569 ft.) and Caudale Moor. The height and steepness of these enclosing fells give a sombre, secluded appearance to the upper part of the vale. From the deep hollow of the northern extremity, and occupying much of its space, rises **Troutbeck Tongue** (1,191 ft.), at the foot, or tip, of which stands a solitary farmstead, the last dwelling in this direction till the summit of Kirkstone has been gained.

The eastern branch of the stream flows between the so-called **Park** and the **Yoke** mountain through a narrow valley called **Hag Ghyll**; and there forms **Hag Ghyll Force,** a waterfall worthy of being better known, but not very easy to see, owing to trees.

12. **Kentmere.** It is best to take the lane past the Windermere Reservoir and climb the Garburn Pass. There are beautiful views of the Troutbeck valley and, after the summit has been reached, of Kentmere itself. The foot of the Pass is close to Kentmere Hall, a farmhouse formerly the home of the Gilpins, the most notable of whom was Bernard Gilpin, "a pious divine called the Apostle of the North" in the reign of Bloody Mary. The church is ancient and overlooks the lower part of the valley where the *mere* was until it was drained more than a hundred years ago. The road along the upper part of the valley is poor (and a cul-de-sac), but walkers will be rewarded by seeing the splendid Rainsborrow Crag, falling almost sheer from Yoke.

AMBLESIDE

Approach.—For **Road Routes** *see* **p. 9.** Rail to Windermere, thence by road (5 miles—frequent bus service). Express coach services from London, Manchester and Liverpool.

Banks.—*National Westminster; Barclays* and *Midlands.*

Boats.—Motor-boats, including jet speed boats, and rowing boats for hire.

Bowls.—At Rothay Holme. Counci green at White Platts.

Buses.—Continuous service to Windermere, Grasmere, Keswick, Coniston, Dungeon Ghyll and Hawkshead.

Car Parking Places.—Waterhead, King Street, Lake Road and Low Fold.

Cinema.—Assembly Rooms, every night of the week.

Early Closing.—Thursday (winter only).

Hotels.—In Ambleside: *Salutation, White Lion, Vale View, Wansfell Tower, Rothay Garth, Fisherbeck, Gables, Rothay Manor.* At Waterhead (on lake): *Waterhead, Tyson's Wateredge, Regent, Romney.* At Rydal: *Glen Rothay.* At Skelwith: *Skelwith Bridge.*

Places of Worship.—*St. Mary's, St. Mary s* (Rydal), *Holy Trinity* (Brathay), *Roman Catholic* (Wansfell Road), *Methodist* (Millans Park).

Post Office.—Market Place.

Boat Pier at Waterhead, about three-quarters of a mile south of town.

Sports.—Annually on Thursday before first Monday in August.

Tennis, Bowls and Putting.—On Recreation Ground close to St. Mary's Church.

Ambleside is built on a lower ledge of Wansfell, on the border of a well-wooded valley watered by several streams, of which the principal is the *Rothay*, which flows from Grasmere and Rydal lakes and joins the *Brathay*, from Langdale, shortly before entering Windermere. It is a very good centre for excursions, particularly for motoring, and there is an abundance of hotels and lodgings.

The parish church, St. Mary's, is a large building of local stone, erected in 1854. It has a stained-glass window in memory of Wordsworth, presented by English and American admirers. There is also a Wordsworth Chapel. There is another window in memory of Matthew Arnold, while a rush-bearing mural painting (1944) attracts attention. The annual Rush-bearing Ceremony takes place each year on a Saturday in the month of July. A similar ceremony takes place at Grasmere early in August. The church has a peal of eight bells, the finest in the county.

At the other end of the village is the **Bridge House** (National Trust), a quaint building over the Stock Beck, probably dating from the seventeenth century.

Waterhead (three-quarters of a mile to the south) is the headquarters of boating on the upper end of the Lake, and the northern terminus of the boat services (*see* p. 55).

Between Waterhead and Rothay Bridge the site of a Roman Camp has been excavated and its foundations laid bare. The site belongs to the National Trust and is open to the public. Pottery, shoes, buttons and tools, have been found.

WALKS ROUND AMBLESIDE

1. To Stock Ghyll Force

The fall is about half a mile from the town. The way to it leads uphill past the *Salutation Hotel* and then through the park entrance on the left.

Stock Ghyll rises on Red Screes (2,541 ft.), the mountain which towers above the Kirkstone Pass. Passing through Ambleside, the stream joins the Rothay a quarter of a mile below the town, after a course of about four miles. This ghyll is one of the finest of its kind in the district. The fall is very attractive, the water tumbling down the face of a rock, through a mountain glen clothed with trees and ferns, and then running among loose rocks and overhanging foliage. The water takes three leaps, being divided by projecting rocks; the total height is seventy feet. The falls are perhaps better seen from below. More than one accident having occurred here, railings have been erected for safety.

After visiting the Ghyll, one may continue up the road and visit either **Wansfell** (p. 80) or the **Kirkstone Pass** (p. 78) by the Grove Farm.

2. To Jenkin Crag

This short stroll should by no means be omitted. Signboards give direction from the east side of the Windermere main road. Where the path forks, keep to the right. From Jenkin Crag a track leads through a wood to High Skelghyll and Troutbeck, or a descent may be made to the main road at Low Wood.

3. Scandale by High Sweden Bridge, returning by Low Sweden Bridge

From the market cross take the Kirkstone road nearly to the Old Church and turn left at a finger-post. Charming views over Rydal Vale are to be had during the outward walk. Round about Sweden Bridge and Scandale Beck the scenery, with foliage, water, and mountain peeps, is very attractive. Distance, four miles.

4. Skelwith Force and Elterwater

The road runs through Clappersgate and thence up the beautiful Brathay valley. A little more than a mile beyond Clappersgate we turn left to **Skelwith Bridge** (*Hotel*) close to which is **Skelwith Force.** Though not one of the large falls of Lakeland, its volume after heavy rain is considerable. Continuing by the riverside, a track leads us across fields and by the much underrated Elterwater to the Britannia Inn. The views of Wetherlam and the Langdale Pikes on this route are unsurpassed. The road walk is somewhat inferior in this respect.

A mile south of Elterwater village is **Colwith Force,** one of the finest series of falls in the district. Approach to it, however, is best made from the Skelwith Bridge–Coniston road.

5. To Rydal and Grasmere

A charming alternative as far as Pelter Bridge is the route described in Excursion 6.

Leaving Ambleside by the Keswick road, we note over the Stock Ghyll stream the old *Bridge House.* A few hundred yards beyond, to the left, is the **Knoll,** where Harriet Martineau used to live, and where she was visited by Charlotte Brontë and George Eliot. Proceeding, we pass on the right Rydal Hall, for many centuries the seat of the le Fleming family. It is now a conference house and surrounded by beautifully-wooded grounds, through which the *Rydal Beck* makes its way to the Rothay. **Pelter Bridge** is the central feature of a pretty roadside scene.

To the left is the sweet **Vale of Rydal,** backed by the many-hued mass of Loughrigg. Here, close to a sharp bend in the stream (the Rothay) is Fox How, where Dr. Arnold, the great Rugby master, lived, but it is not visible from the main road.

After passing through the hamlet of Rydal, the road skirts the northerly margin of—

Rydal Water

one of the smallest, but also one of the most attractive of the lakes. It is not, however, seen to the best advantage from the road. Good peeps at the lake and vale may be obtained from the footpath which starts from behind Rydal Church (*Variation* 1, p. 64), and the track along the other side of the lake, under Loughrigg Fell, reached by a footbridge close to the *Glen Rothay Hotel,* as indicated on p. 64, does justice to the beauties of this little mere, of which the traveller on the high road is hardly aware.

About two hundred yards beyond the last house on the Keswick side of Rydal village is a low rock called **Wordsworth's Seat,** the top of which is reached by a few steps. A short distance nearer Grasmere, the main road has been "by-passed" in front of a roadside cottage on the right. This is **the Nab,** where De Quincey resided for some time, ultimately marrying the daughter of old Simpson, the farmer-occupier of the cottage, with whom he lodged. The Nab was subsequently the residence of Hartley Coleridge. Here he died, January 6, 1849. He was interred in the south-east angle of Grasmere churchyard. Wordsworth also lies in the same churchyard.

The mountain on our right is Nab Scar; to our left lies Rydal Water, with Loughrigg beyond, over which appear, in the order named, as we walk towards Grasmere, the rocky summit of Harrison Stickle (the most prominent of the Langdale Pikes), the serrated Crinkle Crags, and Pike o' Blisco.

At the head of Rydal Water there is a choice of three roads: the first very rough and steep, winding around the slate quarry; the second smoother and rising at an easier angle; the third, the nearly level and smooth main road. However, pedestrians should take the second, in preference to the main road, not only because it avoids the traffic, but because it affords something of a surprise view of **Grasmere** itself. This little lake is considered by some the prettiest in Lakeland, and certainly it is charming to look at and charming to look from, a beautiful jewel in a beautiful setting.* The fell on the western side of the lake is Silver How, with the wild recesses of Easedale running up to the north-west. Farther north Helm Crag (*see* p. 68), with its fantastic summit, overlooks the main road. The mountain beyond is Steel Fell, and between it and Seat Sandal, which rises opposite, is Dunmail Raise (*see* p. 68), over which peeps for a moment the conical summit of Great Calva, in Skiddaw Forest. Closer at hand Stone Arthur sends down smooth grass slopes of great steepness. A little beyond the highest point of the by-road along which we are walking is the **Wishing Gate,** on the site of the gate of which Wordsworth wrote.

Variation 1 (walk). Turn up past Rydal church, and behind Rydal Mount take a track to the left, leading along the foot of Nab Scar. It is a pleasant stroll, and has the advantage of seclusion. This was Wordsworth's favourite path.

Variation 2 (walk). By Pelter Bridge and Loughrigg Terrace (*see* Route 6 below), and so by the western side of Grasmere. Or the main road may be rejoined by the foot-bridge over the Rothay between Rydal and Grasmere lakes. The terrace route, however, though somewhat longer, is preferable, the scenery being finer throughout. The gradual unfolding of the beauties of Grasmere and its surroundings from Loughrigg Terrace is entrancing.

6. To Loughrigg Fell

The walk round Loughrigg Fell, a rocky, fern-clad plateau commanding extensive views, is one of the finest in the neighbourhood. From Market Place pass St. Mary's Church and take the footpath across Rothay Park to **Miller Bridge.** Crossing this, turn to the right and follow the road northward to **Pelter Bridge.** The ramble up the valley is very enjoyable, the country presenting the appearance of a stately park. We pass in succession Fox How on the right; and Fox Ghyll, Loughrigg Holme, Stepping Stones, Loughrigg Cottage, and Field Foot on the left. **Rydal Hall,** standing in an extensive park, with numerous stately forest trees, and **Rydal Mount** (*open*; from 1813 until his death the home of Wordsworth) are seen from several points along the road. The mountains of Fairfield, Great Rigg, and Nab Scar, on the north-east, and Loughrigg Fell on the western side of the valley, present many fine combinations. On reaching **Pelter Bridge,** we leave it on the right, and on arriving at the top of the track come in view of **Rydal Water.**

Turn to the left, along the northern slope of Loughrigg Fell to

* The "Kelds" in the lake—springs which take longer to freeze over than other water—are a source of danger to bathers and skaters.

Thirlmere (*Valentine*)

The Vale of St. John (*J. Hardman*)

Friar's Crag and Grisedale Pike *(J. Salmon Ltd.)*

Keswick and Derwentwater *(J. Salmon Ltd.)*

Red Bank and then make for home by Loughrigg Tarn and Clappersgate.

The north bank of the Brathay is reached about half a mile east of Skelwith Bridge. Passing through **Clappersgate,** a pretty hamlet situated at the foot of the fell, about a mile west of Ambleside, and crossing the bridge over the Rothay, we are soon home again.

For the conclusion of this walk there are two delightful alternatives:

(*a*) From Loughrigg Tarn turn uphill to the left and cross the shoulder of Loughrigg to Miller Bridge.

(*b*) Cross Skelwith Bridge and return by the other side of the river by Spy Hill and Brathay Church where the river may be re-crossed by a footbridge.

These two routes can be combined in one excursion.

GRASMERE

Banks.—*Barclays, National Westminster.* Mon. and Fri. (winter) and Mon., Tues., Thurs., Fri. (summer).

Boats.—Boats available for hire, but *see* p. 17.

Hotels.—*Prince of Wales; Swan; Dale Lodge; Hollens; Moss Grove; Rothay; Oak Bank; Ben Place; Red Lion; Traveller's Rest, Gold Rill,* etc.

Motor Services to Ambleside and Windermere, also to Keswick.

Motor Trips.—*See* p. 72.

Places of Worship.—*Grasmere Church, Methodist Chapel, R.C. Our Lady of the Wayside,* on Ambleside-Keswick road.

Post Office, in village.

Public Hall.—Broadgate.

Tennis Courts.—Broadgate Meadow.

Youth Hostels. *Thorney How* and *Butharlyp How. High Close* hostel nearby.

The most interesting features of **Grasmere Church** are its heavily timbered roof, described by Wordsworth in "The Excursion", and his memorial tablet in the chancel, with its epitaph by John Keble. Wordsworth, with many other members of his family, is buried in the south-east corner of the churchyard, and the graves of Hartley Coleridge and Sir John Richardson, the explorer, are near by.

The ancient custom of *Rush-bearing*, observed annually on the Saturday nearest August 5th, has been maintained for many centuries. Before the church floor was paved, rushes were used for keeping the feet of worshippers warm, and each summer were freshly gathered for the purpose. The ceremony begins at 5 p.m. with a procession round the village, headed by the choir and village band; children carry "bearings" of rushes and flowers, which are then borne into church where the floor is strewn with rushes and a short service held. Three special hymns, recalling the custom and the dedication (to St. Oswald, King of Northumbria) are used.

From the church we pass along the old Rydal road to the main Ambleside–Keswick highway, on the far side of which is the lane containing—

Dove Cottage and Wordsworth Museum

(Admission.—Dove Cottage, *10p.*, Museum, *10p.*, Combined tickets, *16p.*)

Dove Cottage is open daily, in summer, 10–1, 2–6 (closed on Sundays); in winter 10–1, 2–4.30 (closed mid-January to 1 March).

Museum open in summer, except Sundays. Closed in winter.

At Dove Cottage, Wordsworth lived on his first settlement at Grasmere in 1799. The house still presents the same appearance. Here again we have many associations with the literary giants of the past. Here we find Wordsworth and his sister, with De Quincey as a guest; and from the latter, who himself afterwards lived for many years in the cottage, we have a number of reminiscences of the days spent at Grasmere. The relics preserved in the Cottage and Museum include some manuscripts of Wordsworth's poems, a large number of portraits of Wordsworth, his family, and of nearly all his friends. Most of the furniture has special interest in connection with Wordsworth. The Museum also contains objects illustrating old Westmorland life.

William Wordsworth was born at Cockermouth (*see* p. 141) on April 7, 1770. After his mother's death in 1778 he, with a brother, was sent to Hawkshead's famous Grammar School (*see* p. 73), and spent five years there. In 1783 his father's death broke up the Cockermouth home, and Wordsworth lived mainly at Penrith, before going to Cambridge where he graduated in 1791.

For a time he settled with his sister Dorothy at Racedown, near Crewkerne from which they moved to Alfoxden in Somerset to be near Coleridge who was collaborating in the *Lyrical Ballads*.

The poet and his sister entered Dove Cottage, near Grasmere, at the end of 1799. In the white-walled cottage the poet's genius flourished. Here were written *The Green Linnet*, *Michael*, *The Daffodils*, *The Ode on the Intimations of Immortality* (a piece of introspective thought which has never been excelled), and such longer pieces as *The Prelude*, and the beginning of *The Excursion*. To Dove Cottage, in 1802, Wordsworth brought his bride, and here three of their five children were born. In 1808 the family removed across the valley to Allan Bank, De Quincey taking the cottage, and in 1811 to the rectory of Grasmere, opposite the old church of St. Oswald. In another two years the deaths of two children sent them to the sanctuary of Rydal Mount.

In 1843, on the death of Southey, Wordsworth was appointed Poet Laureate, and seven years later (April 23, 1850) he died. His sister Dorothy, whose shrewd sense and ability had kept guard on the poet's life, survived until 1855, and Mrs. Wordsworth until 1859. They are all buried in Grasmere churchyard, within sound of their beloved Rothay.

The Grasmere Sports, the event of the season, take place usually on the third Thursday after the first Monday in August. Wrestling is perhaps the chief attraction, but in popularity it is closely run by the "Guides' Race" and the "Hound Trail."

WALKS ROUND GRASMERE

1. To Easedale Tarn. Follow the road northward from Read's Bookshop by Moss Parrock, and keep left at the fork. On the wall at the fork a tablet directs to Easedale Tarn. From here the road is followed till a footbridge on the left is reached. We cross this and take the track by Sour Milk Ghyll to the tarn, 915 feet above sea-level. The excursion, though short, is most picturesque.

2. Round the Lakes. Follow the Ambleside road as far as the foot-bridge at the foot of Rydal Water; then, crossing the Rothay, return by Loughrigg Terrace along the far side of the lakes, rejoining the road from Langdale to Grasmere at Red Bank. If the round of Grasmere only is contemplated, the Ambleside road should be left at the bridge between the two lakes. Total round about six miles.

3. Grisedale Tarn by Tongue Ghyll. Follow the Keswick road for a mile and a half and then take the turning on the right, for **Tongue Ghyll.** A short distance up on the right is **Tongue Ghyll Force,** pretty, but difficult of access.

About half a mile from the main road, after crossing a bridge the path divides. Follow the left-hand track. From this point it is nearly all uphill till the head of the pass comes in sight, when a little more rough going brings **Grisedale Tarn** into view. We are now on the slope of Seat Sandal, which rises to the left of and behind us; Fairfield is on our right; and on the far side of the tarn is Dollywaggon Pike, with the Helvellyn track zigzagging steeply up it.

It is worth while walking to the outlet of the tarn and looking down the pass in the direction of Patterdale. About a hundred yards from Grisedale Tarn, at the head of Grisedale, is **The Brothers' Parting,** so called because here, in 1805, the poet bade a last farewell to his brother, John Wordsworth, who was shortly afterwards drowned in the wreck of his ship, the *Earl of Abergavenny*, off Southampton. Wordsworth commemorated the event in some verses, two of which were cut in the rock face through the enterprise of the late Canon Rawnsley.

Returning, an unexpected view of the fells beyond Derwentwater is obtained between Seat Sandal and Dollywaggon.

4. Round Thirlmere. (The Ambleside–Keswick buses pass along the road on the eastern side of the Lake.)

Taking the Keswick road we begin, as soon as we leave the village, the steep ascent of **Dunmail Raise,** which looks down upon Grasmere. The summit, 783 feet above sea-level, is between **Steel Fell** on the west and **Seat Sandal** on the east.

The tumulus or cairn is reputed to mark the burial-place of Dunmail, last king of Cumberland, who fell in battle 945.

On the way up the pass **Helm Crag** (1,299 ft., 1,100 ft. higher than Grasmere Lake) specially attracts attention. The rugged rocks of the summit assume a variety of shapes, according to the position from which they are viewed. The most familiar of these is the *Lion and Lamb*, which in due course becomes the *Old Woman at the Organ*.

We now cross the boundary into Cumberland, a mile and a quarter from **Wythburn** with its famous church (*see* p. 97).

For the round of Thirlmere *see* Keswick section, p. 97.

5. To Ambleside by Loughrigg Tarn. Follow the road along the western side of the Lake and over Red Bank and so by Loughrigg Tarn and Clappersgate or by Loughrigg Brow and Miller Bridge (*see* p. 64).

6. To Elterwater by Hunting Stile. On the western side of the Lake, a mile after leaving the village, a track leads over the low elevation to the right by Hunting Stile, rejoining the main road from Langdale to Grasmere below High Close. Elterwater village lies a little beyond.

7. To Dungeon Ghyll. Dungeon Ghyll (*see* p. 51) may be reached from Grasmere by various routes. The simplest way to walk is past Allan Bank, and then by Score Crag. The ridge is crossed at **Yew Crag** (1,345 ft.)—be careful not to walk up Silver How, to the left, by mistake—descending to the road at Pye Howe. A more ambitious route is by Easedale Tarn and Codale Tarn, then over the ridge to Stickle Tarn, and follow the Mill Gill down to the Dungeon Ghyll New Hotel. The return journey is most easily made by Hunting Stile, a preferable route of approach in misty weather.

CONISTON

Approach.—*Rail* to Ulverston or Windermere and then by *bus*.

Road Routes.—*See* p. 9.

Banks.—*National Westminster, Barclays.*

Boating.—Small boats for hire.

Bowls.—Yewdale Road.

Hotels.—*Sun; Crown; Black Bull; Ship Inn.*

Places of Worship.—*Parish Church, Roman Catholic Church, Methodist Chapel.*

Stations.—Ulverston (14 m.), Foxfield (10 m.).

Tennis and Putting.—Yewdale Road.

The village lies near the western shore of Coniston Water, at the northern end. It is a pleasant place for a summer sojourn, and a very fair centre for excursions.

The **Ruskin Museum,** about 100 yards from the church on the Yewdale Road, contains Ruskin pictures, relics and MSS. and articles illustrating the history of Coniston.

The **Church,** plain and unpretentious, contains in its peaceful "God's acre" the **Grave of John Ruskin** (d. January 20, 1900). At the head of the grave stands a tall cross of grey-green slate stone, quarried from the neighbouring vale of Tilberthwaite. The sculpture is illustrative of Ruskin's chief works. The original church was consecrated in 1586 (prior to which date the district was in the parish of Ulverston) and the present church was built in 1819. In the baptistery there is a small window by Kempe worthy of notice.

Coniston Water

Coniston Water is five and a quarter miles long and half a mile wide. Its banks are beautifully wooded and on its surface are two pretty islets, **Peel Island** and **Fir Island** (both National Trust). Between Lake Bank and Waterhead, we obtain fine views of the Old Man, Dow Crags above Goats Water, Yewdale and Tilberthwaite, Helvellyn, Fairfield and Red Screes. Small boats are available for hire. It was on Coniston Water in January 1967 that the late Donald Campbell made his tragic 300 mph water speed record run in his ill-fated "Bluebird". A memorial to him stands in the village.

WALKS ROUND CONISTON

1. To Tarn Hows

Follow the Hawkshead road running close to the lake, and take the second turning to the left, a wooded lane, with charming retrospective views of Coniston Water. (If transport is taken, the Tarn must be approached by High Cross.) Later the prospect opens finely to the left over Yewdale. Walk up the bracken-covered slope to the right, from which the Coniston district is well seen. A short distance farther we come somewhat suddenly on the lakelet of **Tarn Hows,** as pretty a picture as ever delighted the eye. Although it is now one sheet of water it used to be three and is still sometimes known as "the Tarns" and, to add to the confusion, maps have marked it as "Highlow Tarn". Most of the surrounding countryside belongs to the National Trust.

The return should be made by descending the picturesque *Tom Ghyll* or Glen Mary—the opening of which enframes a striking silhouette of the distant Langdale Pikes—and by the Coniston-Ambleside road, which is reached close to Yew Tree Farm. From the next farm, High Yewdale, there is a footpath through fields nearly to the village. The round is not much over five miles.

2. To Tilberthwaite

Take the road to Yewdale. At a signpost about 1½ miles from Coniston the Tilberthwaite road forks to the left, and in another mile a path strikes off to the left again about 250 yards short of a group of cottages. (Cars may be left here.) The lower end of the path is by no means promising, climbing an untidy pile of debris from the quarries, but presently the steep-sided glen is well seen. Land-slips and quarries notwithstanding, Tilberthwaite Ghyll is worth visiting.

3. Round the Lake

The circuit of the Lake can be made on foot, and there are good views throughout, but on the return along the eastern shore those of the Coniston Fells to the left and the Fairfield and Helvellyn ranges in front are particularly attractive. *Brantwood*, towards the northern end of the Lake, was for over a quarter of a century the home of John Ruskin. The great writer died here. In 1933 the Brantwood estate was acquired as a permanent memorial of Ruskin and is run as a centre for Adult Education. The house contains many articles associated with Ruskin and is open to the public *daily*, 10–4.30. Small charge. Coniston Village is regained by following the road close to the north tip of the lake.

4. To Grizedale

By bus or boat to Lake Bank. Thence walk down the River Crake till you cross it at Low Nibthwaite. Returning by the opposite bank, strike up to the right at High Nibthwaite, keeping almost parallel with the lake-side for about two miles. After crossing the moor, the village of Grizedale appears in the valley below. Do not descend to the houses but bear left by a rough road which runs diagonally north-west across Coniston Moor and terminates near the head of Coniston Water. The total distance is about fifteen miles. Grizedale is prettily wooded. It belongs to the Forestry Commission. There is a Deer Museum, marked nature trail, picnic site and camp site. Visitors are advised to keep to the marked paths. Fine views on the return descent to Coniston.

5. To Hawkshead

From the village take the Hawkshead road, running close to the northern end of the Lake, of which there are exquisite views. Two miles from Coniston, at High Cross, fork right to Hawkshead Hill where there is a Baptist Chapel. 250 yards farther a footpath strikes off on the right and is to be preferred to the road, unless it is desired to see Hawkshead Hall (p. 73).

6. The Duddon Valley

(For motorists the road is narrow beyond Seathwaite. The surface is fairly good and the route leads over Wrynose to Little Langdale.)

Take a bus down to *Broughton-in-Furness.* Thence the route lies up the valley of the Duddon, a river which rises on Wrynose, close to the "Three-Shire Stones." The river was rendered classic by Wordsworth, who made it the subject of no fewer than thirty-four sonnets. It runs through wild and picturesque country; and the scenery will amply recompense those who wander along its course. At **Duddon Bridge** either side of the stream may be taken as far as Ulpha. The usual road is the one on the east and is preferable for scenery. At **Ulpha** (*Traveller's Rest Inn*) a road strikes off steeply to the west and goes over Birker Moor to Eskdale. In another two miles the river is again crossed in order to reach—

Seathwaite*

an attractively-situated hamlet (*Newfield Inn*). Passing the junction of Seathwaite Beck with the Duddon, and turning an elbow of the road we reach the former parsonage and the little **Church**, occupying the site of the old chapel which was the scene of the ministrations of "Wonderful Walker".

The **Rev. Robert Walker** has, through the writings of Wordsworth, attained almost world-wide celebrity. He was curate of Seathwaite for sixty-seven years and though his stipend was extremely low by dint of honest endeavour he managed to leave quite a small fortune. His grave is within a few yards of a yew-tree, more than two hundred years old, around which he was in the habit of assembling his flock, and ministering to their bodily wants between the services on Sundays.

The present church is very different from the "lowly house of prayer" (school, wool-store and "spinning-mill" combined), although Ruskin and others tried their best to have the old building preserved as a memorial.

From Seathwaite the walker's route back to Coniston is by the mountain track over **Walna Scar,** a somewhat weary journey at the end of a long day. (Total distance 13 miles.)

This route may be taken the reverse way, returning from Broughton by car. This alternative is to be recommended on account of the magnificent surprise view of Scafell and the western fells on reaching the top of Walna Scar. A mile below Seathwaite a pretty road swings over the fell to Broughton Mills and Broughton, saving a mile or so in distance.

* It will be to the advantage of the tourist to remember that in the Lake District many places far apart bear identical names. There are, for instance, two well-known Seathwaites (this and the one in Borrowdale), several Mosedales, about half a score Sour Milk Ghylls, and almost countless Raven Crags.

LONGER EXCURSIONS IN THE SOUTHERN AREA

The following are popular excursions laid on by the rail, boat and coach concerns, and as they introduce the principal features of the district the routes should be studied by motorists. Walkers should bear in mind that there are bus services on nearly all these routes, enabling one to break journey at any point desired.

1. WINDERMERE TO KESWICK

The road from Windermere to Keswick is the busiest in the Lake District. It is very pretty in parts—as in the neighbourhood of Rydal and Grasmere—and almost throughout its length commands good views. Current details are widely advertised. Descriptions of the various features passed *en route* will readily be found with the aid of the Index. The route is outlined on pp. 47–8.

2. WINDERMERE — THE FERRY — HAWKSHEAD — CONISTON — SKELWITH — WATERHEAD, AND BACK

From the Ferry a steep ascent takes us through the two hamlets of **Sawrey.** At Near Sawrey is Beatrix Potter's home, Hill Top Farm (N.T. Easter to end October weekdays 11–5.30, Sundays 2–5.30. Adults, 15p. Children 2½p.) which contains an interesting collection of her possessions. Continuing we reach—

Esthwaite Water

a prettily situated little lake, about two miles long and half a mile broad at its widest part. A small round pond at its head is known as the **Priest's Pot**. Harriet Martineau says that by some people the strange name is accounted for by "a tradition that a priest was drowned there; and by others by a supposition of its holding about as much as a thirsty priest would like to drink, if the liquor were sufficiently good." Esthwaite Water flows into Windermere by the *Cunsey Beck*. It holds some trout, but more perch and pike; no char are to be found in it, though the larger lake, close by, is famous for those fish. From the road along the eastern side of Esthwaite Water there are fine views ahead of the Coniston Fells, the Bowfell range, and the Langdale Pikes.

Just beyond the head of the Lake is—

Hawkshead

now a village, though once a county town (*Queen's Head, Red Lion, Sun, Ivy House, Drunken Duck* (2½ m.).) The older part is picturesque and extremely interesting. Many of the houses have been enlarged by having extensions built on to them, with little or no regard for adjacent roads and paths, so that one passes from space to space by means of "tunnels" or narrow lanes. The whole is strongly reminiscent of Robin Hood's Bay or Polperro, except, of course, that the nearest sheet of water is half a mile away, and Hawkshead is fresh and clean and lovely with flowers.

The most interesting building in Hawkshead, however, is the **Grammar School,** which was founded in 1585 by Edwin Sandys, Archbishop of York. Wordsworth was educated here, and on one of the forms is the poet's name, said to have been cut by himself. There is a small admission charge.

The **Church** (St. Michael's), overlooks the village on the south. There was a church here in Norman times, but notwithstanding the appearance of some of the nave pillars (with neither base nor capital) it is almost certain that as a whole the present building dates from the fifteenth century. In the north-east corner is an interesting altar-tomb (1578) to William and Margaret Sandys; note also the dug-out muniments chest (1603) in the St. James's Chapel.

About 600 yards north of the village, at the bridge where the Ambleside and Coniston roads divide and close to Hawkshead Hall (a farmhouse) is an old building, formerly a **Court House** of the monks of Furness Abbey. It is an oblong structure, and was approached by steps. Underneath is a fine arched gateway over which is a niche intended for an image. Looking south is a mullioned window, filled with tracery. The building (National Trust) is used as a studio and is open in summer at reasonable times.

By reason of the views, the field-path between Hawkshead and the Baptist Chapel at Hawkshead Hill is even more remunerative when followed in a westerly direction than as an approach to Hawkshead. The prospect from the brow of the hill over towards Fairfield is superb.

From the top of Hawkshead Hill onwards the Coniston range is the attraction till the road descends steeply a richly wooded slope, affording occasional glimpses of lake and mountain. The road almost touches the water at the head of Coniston before reaching Coniston village.

The return route from Coniston to Windermere is through **Yewdale.**

About a mile and a half from Coniston we pass the turning for **Tilberthwaite,** and a little farther on is **Yew Tree Farm** and then **Yew Tree Tarn,** an artificial lakelet which nevertheless embellishes the scenery. At the top of the ascent from Coniston, at Oxenfell Cross, a mountain road crosses the motor road. The left-hand branch leads back to Coniston by Hodge Close and Tilberthwaite. The right-hand crosses the fells behind Tarn Hows and joins the Ambleside road to Coniston, *via* Barn Gates and High Cross, at Borwick Lodge. Taken the reverse way from Borwick Lodge, this is unequalled amongst the road-walks of the District. Soon after this the prospect opens to the left, affording occasional glimpses of the Langdale Pikes, followed, on the descent to the Brathay, by a grand panorama extending from Wetherlam and Bowfell to High Street and Ill Bell. (For **Skelwith,** *see* p. 62.)

3. THE ROUND OF THE LANGDALES FROM AMBLESIDE

The road from Great Langdale to Little Langdale provides a thoroughly enjoyable route for the walker. In the reverse direction it is doubtful whether the surprise view as one climbs from Little Langdale to Blea Tarn and descends into

Great Langdale is a worthy exchange for the magnificent scene that greets those travelling *up* Great Langdale. It is a predicament that is best solved by making the round twice —once in each direction.

4. TO FURNESS ABBEY

The direct road route from Windermere is *via* Newby Bridge, Greenodd, Ulverston and Dalton. The return should be varied by taking the road from Greenodd to Coniston, whence the way to Ambleside has already been described.

FURNESS ABBEY

Open 10–4.30 Nov.–Feb., 9.30–5.30 Mar., April, Oct., 7 p.m. May–Sept. Sundays from 2 Oct.–April, 9.30 May–Sept. Admission charge.

The Abbey was founded by Stephen, Count of Mortain and Boulogne, afterwards King of England. The monks were of the Order of Savigny in Normandy, an offshoot from the Benedictine Order founded about 1112, some thirteen years after the establishment of the Cistercian Order. They had first settled in 1123 at Tulketh near Preston, but moved to Furness in 1127. A few years later the Savigny monasteries adopted the Cistercian rule, and Furness, somewhat reluctantly, followed suit.

The abbot exercised vice-regal power, had the assize of bread and ale throughout the district, Aldingham and Ulverston excepted, the appointment of chief constable for the Liberty, free chase through all the district, and wrecks of sea on the coast, except in Aldingham.

For the maintenance of his power and prerogatives, as well as for the defence of the coast and castle of Piel, he kept up a numerous retinue of servants and armed followers. The abbots of Furness were lords in Parliament, but owing to the isolated situation of the abbey, the dangerous nature of the roads and the distance from the metropolis, they do not appear to have sat in the great council of the kingdom, although several times summoned. The privileges and estates of the abbey were confirmed by twelve successive kings.

So large were the possessions of this establishment, in this and other counties, and to such an extent did its opulence augment, that it was surpassed by no Cistercian house in the kingdom, except Fountains Abbey in Yorkshire.

Close to the station is the **Gateway Chapel,** forty-nine feet long by twenty-eight wide.

By following the road the visitor is led to a full view of the church. Some 300 yards beyond is a swing gate where the admission fee is paid. The semi-circular doorway which forms the principal entrance opens into the north transept.

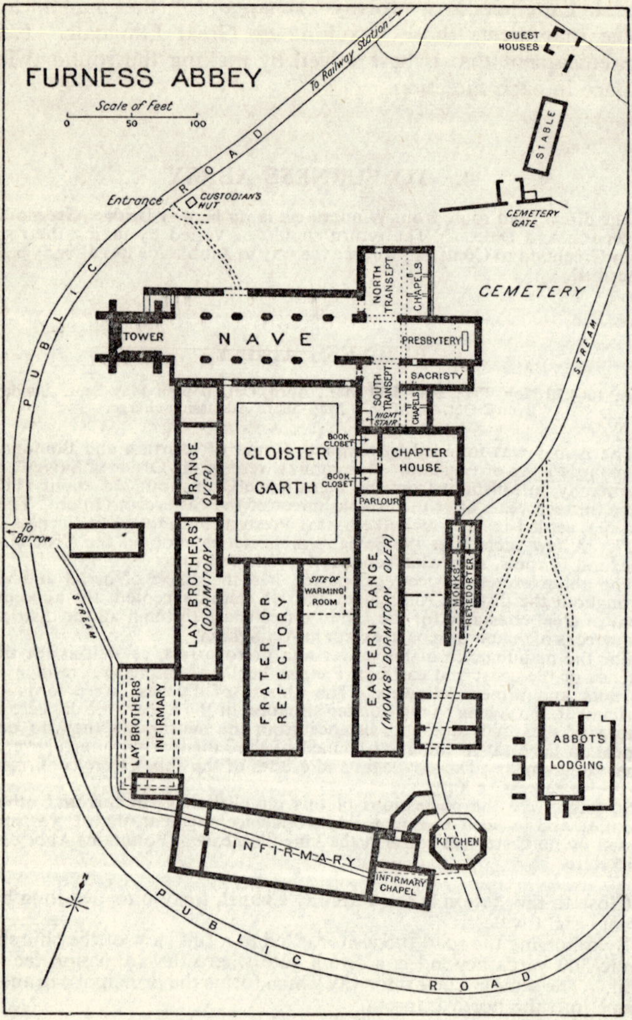
FURNESS ABBEY
Scale of Feet
0
50
100
To Railway Station
GUEST HOUSES
STABLE
Entrance
CUSTODIAN'S HUT
PUBLIC ROAD
CEMETERY GATE
CEMETERY
NORTH TRANSEPT
CHAPELS
TOWER
NAVE
PRESBYTERY
SACRISTY
SOUTH TRANSEPT
CHAPELS
NIGHT STAIR
BOOK CLOSET
CLOISTER GARTH
CHAPTER HOUSE
BOOK CLOSET
PARLOUR
STREAM
RANGE OVER)
LAY BROTHERS' (DORMITORY
To Barrow
STREAM
SITE OF WARMING ROOM
FRATER OR REFECTORY
EASTERN RANGE (MONKS' DORMITORY OVER)
MONKS' REREDORTER
LAY BROTHERS' INFIRMARY
ABBOTS LODGING
INFIRMARY
KITCHEN
INFIRMARY CHAPEL
PUBLIC ROAD

The Church,

built, as usual, in the form of a cross, possessed various sub-divisions, and from the portions still visible an accurate idea of its proportions and limits can be gained.

The **Western Tower,** or Belfry, is of later date than the rest, belonging apparently to the latter part of the fifteenth or the early part of the sixteenth century, when the Perpendicular style had taken the place of the Decorated. The walls, eleven feet thick, are strengthened with six-staged buttresses.

Inside, the tower measures twenty-four feet by nineteen. The splendid Perpendicular west window, with splays decorated with the leaf-like ornament of that period was thirty-five feet high and eleven and a half wide.

The **Transept,** dividing the chancel from the nave, measures a hundred and twenty-nine feet by twenty-eight, the walls composing it being from four to six feet thick, and of their original height. The chapels were those of the Lancasters, barons of Kendal, who were great benefactors to the abbey.

In the **North Transept** was a window, thirty feet high and seventeen and a half wide, and in the south wall another, seventeen and a half feet by twelve feet, both showing the substitution of the Perpendicular style for that preceding it. Over the centre was the lantern tower, supported by four noble arches. The eastern of these remains, from the floor to the under side of the apex is fifty-two and a half feet.

The **Chancel** was lighted by four lofty windows, in addition to the magnificent east window, which, when perfect, was forty-seven feet in height and twenty-three and a half across.

The external mouldings of the great chancel window are supported on each side by crowned heads, possibly meant to represent Stephen, the founder, and Maud, his wife. In the south wall of the chancel are the combined **Sedilia** and **Piscina,** executed in the most exquisite Perpendicular style.

The Conventual Buildings

The Conventual Buildings are grouped round the **Cloister,** and the principal rooms, as usual, were on the east. Here attention is at once arrested by five richly-moulded semi-circular arches, with dog-toothed moulding. The middle archway forms an open porch, with groined and vaulted roof, the sides having been originally ornamented with marble columns supporting an arcade of six trefoil-headed niches. This archway forms the entrance to the **Chapter House,** whose vaulted roof, long fallen in, was supported by two rows of slender fluted columns. More decoration appears to have been lavished on this apartment and the chancel of the church than on any other part of the abbey buildings.

The next arch, less elaborate, leads into the **Parlour,** the only place where conversation was permitted. The similar arch next to it opens into a chamber which measures two hundred feet in length by thirty-one feet in breadth. It had a vaulted roof, groined from the corbels still visible, to the heavy eight-sided columns, whose bases remain on the floor. Above this vaulted undercroft was the Monks' Dormitory.

The South Side of the cloister-court was occupied by the warming-room and the **Frater,** or common eating-hall, and the West Side by the buildings devoted to the lay brothers. Only the foundations of all these buildings remain.

Beyond the Dormitory to the south is the *Infirmary*, with chapel and domestic offices attached. The vestibule has several entrances, with staircases in the wall leading to the rooms above. With the adjoining chapel it is the only portion of the conventual buildings with roof entire, and affords a good example of the groined vaulting of the period. The chapel is now protected by an iron gate and serves as a repository for relics found among the ruins, many curious gargoyles, corbels, mouldings, and other interesting remains being here collected, including two early effigies from tombs. To the north-east of the Infirmary is another smaller group, the Abbot's Lodging, rebuilt and altered from the original Infirmary.

From the remains of the monastic buildings a footpath leads to an eminence from which an excellent bird's-eye view is obtained of the abbey and its domain.

In 1896–7, in the course of extensive excavations, a papal bulla, or leaden seal, was discovered, dating from the thirteenth century. The seal had been attached to one of the five Bulls sent to the Cistercian establishment at Furness in the time of Pope Innocent IV (1243–1254), while William de Middleton was Abbot.

5. PATTERDALE BY THE KIRKSTONE PASS AND BACK

The distance from Ambleside to Patterdale by Kirkstone Pass is ten miles from Windermere a very long fourteen (for route from Windermere by Troutbeck, *see* p. 59).

From Ambleside one almost immediately begins the ascent of—

Kirkstone Pass

and the walker is recommended to take the Stock Ghyll route (p. 62) in preference to the main road, which is steeper and less interesting. *Cars should go by Troutbeck.* The pass is between **Red Screes** and **Caudale Moor.** About two hundred yards short of the summit is a small public-house, the *Kirkstone Pass Inn* (1,468 ft. above sea-level), asserted to be the highest licensed house in the kingdom, though there are two higher: "Tan Hill" in Yorkshire (1,727 ft.), the highest, and the "Cat and Fiddle" near Buxton. On the left, Red Screes rises with striking steepness.

Descending the other side, we see, on the left, the Kirk Stone, a large detached rock which, according to popular fancy, "gives the savage pass its name." The lofty mountains on both sides are covered with fragments of rock, and a little stream runs wildly down the pass, receiving accessions from numerous rivulets. Descending steeply—*motorists, and especially cyclists, beware!*—we come in sight of—

Brothers' Water

with the heights of Patterdale in the distance. The legend is that at the beginning of the nineteenth century on two separate occasions two brothers were drowned here in winter by the breaking of the ice.

The road runs along the east side of Brothers' Water, and then turns sharp to the left across the meadows and then right, leaving Dovedale behind. Three-quarters of a mile farther on the romantic **Deepdale** runs up into the mountains on the left, revealing some fine precipices. Following the *Goldrill Beck,* we come first to **Patterdale** and so to Glenridding and the *Ullswater Hotel.* Allow time for a steamer trip up and down the Lake; an alternative is to use the bus as far as Pooley Bridge, return to Patterdale by boat and thence to Ambleside by bus by way of Windermere station. (A regular service operates over Kirkstone Pass in summer time.)

The Fells (Southern Section)

Windermere is the starting-point for the Ill Bell group. The Red Screes and Fairfield range belong equally to Ambleside and Grasmere. Grasmere has also a claim on Helvellyn and practically the monopoly of the Langdale Pikes; and Coniston has exclusive possession of the Old Man group. **Loughrigg,** the long low fell that lies between Windermere and Grasmere, can be ascended from almost any direction, by various footpaths.

1. Wansfell Pike

This is the height to the north-east of Ambleside. There are three routes to the top; perhaps the best is that which combines with a visit to **Stock Ghyll Force** (*see* p. 62). Having viewed the fall, we retrace our steps to the entrance gate, turn to the left, and in about five minutes pass through a gate which crosses the road. In a few hundred yards an iron step-stile will be seen, by means of which we gain the pasture on the right. The way to the summit is now straight ahead, but steep. **Wansfell Pike** is 1,587 ft. above sea-level, and 1,400 ft. higher than Ambleside. Perhaps no view of Windermere, with its numerous wood-clad islets, is more charming.

The fine mountain screen which surrounds the Lake forms the background of the view; the valleys of the Brathay and Rothay may be traced from the sources of those rivers to the spot where they fall, as one stream, into the lake; and Ambleside, Rydal, Grasmere, Wray Castle, and many other delectable places may be clearly seen. The mountain panorama is extensive and impressive. The low, rounded fell, away to the west by the sea, is Black Combe; as we turn to our right we come to the Coniston range, and then Crinkle Crags, Bowfell, and the Langdale Pikes. Peeps of Scafell and Scafell Pike are visible on either side of Bowfell. Beyond this point the northern fells somewhat interfere with the view, although Red Screes, with Hart Crag and Fairfield, form an imposing barrier, and the ridges and valleys descending from them to the south are seen to great advantage. To the east are the High Street and Ill Bell ranges.

To return we make our way eastwards to Nanny Lane, which leads us from the Hundreds, a subordinate elevation of Wansfell 1,250 ft. high, to the village of Troutbeck, and then, following the high road as far as the Institute, turn along a branch road in a north-westerly direction. Crossing the Holbeck, we can pause for a time at **High Skelgill**, gaining a pretty glimpse of **Pull Wyke Bay** and its lovely surroundings, and in due time re-enter Ambleside by Jenkin Crag (p. 62).

2. Ill Bell, Froswick, Thornthwaite Crag, with Caudale Moor

(*See Outline Guide* (*k*), p. 43)

The ascent is best made from the summit of the Garburn Pass, following the ridge-line over the Yoke, Ill Bell, and Froswick to Thornthwaite Crag.

Steady-headed people may indulge in fine views almost straight down into Kentmere; **Thornthwaite Crag** and **Ill Bell** are the favourite view-points. Windermere is seen almost at its best. Beyond are the Coniston Fells, the Old Man conspicuous by his large cairn. Wetherlam descends grandly to Wrynose, and on the other side the wild Crinkle Crags run up to the graceful peak of Bowfell. Beyond are Scafell and Scafell Pike, with Great Gable to the right. The Langdale Pikes are easily recognisable, though it is hard at first to realise that those comparatively insignificant hills are the peaks that present so striking a front towards Langdale. Fairfield and the Helvellyn range block the view to the north. The Pennines sweep round from east to south, where the flat-topped Ingleborough is readily recognisable.

It is worth while strolling a short distance from the columnar cairn on Thornthwaite Crag in the direction of the Nan Bield Pass for the sake of a charming peep of Hayeswater on the left, and if time permits the walk should certainly be continued to High Street.

The return is usually made by dropping down into Troutbeck (*see* p. 60), in a slanting direction from the depression between Thornthwaite Crag and Froswick. Strong walkers may complete the round by crossing **Caudale Moor** to the Kirkstone Pass. The descent to Thresthwaite Mouth (the *col* between Thornthwaite Crag and Caudale Moor) is very steep and shaky, and the ascent of Caudale Moor a rough clamber. The views on either hand are very attractive. The summit of Red Screes is a guide to the right line from Caudale Moor to Kirkstone. Below on the right are Brothers' Water (*see* p. 79) and the green valley of the Goldrill, which leads to Patterdale. Our course is to keep fairly close to the ridge-line to the head of the Kirkstone Pass, descending a little short of the Inn.

Most walkers will find the complete round a full day's work. The half course, however, can be easily undertaken without excessive hurrying.

3. Red Screes, Dove Crag, Hart Crag, Fairfield, Great Rigg, Nab Scar

(*See Outline Guide* (*i*), p. 42)

(A full eight-hour day should be allowed to do the round leisurely.)

Either of the buttresses of this group may be taken as a separate expedition, Red Screes by Scandale (Scandale Head is abominably marshy) (p. 62), Fairfield preferably from Grisedale Tarn, inasmuch as the slopes above Grasmere are exceedingly steep. As, however, it only takes a very easy two hours to link up the two summits over the tops, with the additional charm of numerous views, it is far preferable to take the whole round. It is best to start from Ambleside.

About a mile along the Kirkstone road a gate on the left opens into a grass lane. This leads on to the ridge-line, which should be followed to the summit, a rather weary grind, as the top is set much farther back than one suspects. Abundant compensation is found in the view, which is superb.

Windermere is well seen, and beyond is Morecambe Bay, looking very attractive on a sunny day. The Windermere fells are close at hand. Immediately below is the Kirkstone Pass. To the north-east is the High Street range, Kidsty Pike conspicuous, with the Pennines and Cross Fell beyond, and near at hand the broken fells round Angle Tarn. There is just a peep of Ullswater to the north-east. Most of the view to the north is shut out by Fairfield and St. Sunday Crag, with Helvellyn beyond. To the east of these is seen a little bit of Saddleback. Westward the mountain panorama extends from the Coniston Fells by Bowfell, Scafell Pike, Great Gable and Pillar to the fells above Derwentwater.

From the Summit of Red Screes, make diagonally for the wall at the head of the Scandale-Caiston *col* (*drinking-water on the way*). Follow the wall and, later, wire fence for a while to the side of Dove Crag, leaving Little Hart Crag on the right. Here is the last drinking-water on the round. The ascent of Dove Crag is also the last bit of collar-work. A glance from its summit reveals that thenceforward the northern sides of the range are mostly precipitous. There is also a fine view of St. Sunday Crag. Return diagonally to the wall. The long ridge to the south is Scandale Fell, leading back to Ambleside. Disregard this and carry on over the rough summit of Hart Crag till Fairfield is reached.

Fairfield itself is a smooth grassy level, the most extensive summit, we believe, in the District, and an easy place to get lost on in a mist. By walking a short way in the direction of Cofa Pike we can look down on Greenhow End, which presents an imposing appearance. To the north Saddleback has disappeared, but close at hand are Striding Edge and the precipices of Helvellyn. In other respects the view is much the same as from Red Screes. There is rather an embarrassment of cairns hereabouts. Remember to face south and keep to the ridge-line. If you find yourself descending to the right, you are wrong. Caution against descending to the left from the ridge is needless. Where the path forks, keep always to the left by Great Rigg, Heron Crag and Lords Pike till Nab Scar is reached. A well-marked descent, very steep, leads down to Rydal, a short distance from the main road and convenient buses.

4. Langdale Pikes

(*See Outline Guide* (*h*), p. 41)

The ascent from the Dungeon Ghyll hotels should be made either by Dungeon Ghyll or Mill Gill; from Grasmere by Blea Rigg. The former is the wilder and grander; the latter affords a more extended prospect. Whatever divergence of opinion there may be on this point, there can be no question that the descent by Dungeon Ghyll should not be attempted in thick weather, and that the descent to Langdale anywhere else along the frontage is absolutely barred. An alternative is to cross the summit of Pavey Ark, descending to the far side of Stickle Tarn, and returning round the Tarn and so by Mill Gill, with the stream on the right. There is a shorter but steeper and rougher descent between Pavey Ark and Harrison Stickle. All that is necessary is to remember that Stickle Tarn (1,540 ft.) comes into sight far below on the left almost at once on commencing the descent, and that the route lies about midway between Harrison Stickle and Pavey Ark. If stopped by rocks, all that is needed is to walk towards the middle of the slope. The use of the hands is never required.

The Pikes command a fine view, but the walker will be well advised to strike north, leaving Pavey Ark on the right, over the open grass slopes for a little more than a mile until the summit of **High Raise** is reached.

The mountain panorama is magnificent—the finest in the whole Lake Country. Starting from the Coniston range (note the peak close to the Old Man; it is Dow Crags, the expert rock-climber's paradise), and turning to the right, we come to Crinkle Crags, Bowfell, which seems to tower over the Langdale Pikes, Scafell and Scafell Pike, Great End, Great Gable, and Pillar. Glaramara is at our feet, with Honister Crag in profile beyond, and beyond again the Buttermere Fells. Next come Dalehead, with the red bulk of Grassmoor behind it, and the Newlands fells, the graceful peak of Grisedale Pike conspicuous. Then, beyond the trench formed by Bassenthwaite Lake, is Criffel, in Kirkcudbrightshire. Next come Skiddaw and Saddleback to the north. On the east is the long Helvellyn range, with Fairfield, Red Screes, and Ill Bell, and farther round is a flat-topped hill, Ingleborough, in Yorkshire. The prospect to the south includes Windermere and Morecambe Bay.

5. Crinkle Crags and Bowfell

(*See Outline Guide* (*e*), p. 38)

Bowfell is, like Great Gable, splendid to look at and splendid to look from. It commands Eskdale, the valley of the Duddon, and Langdale.

The ascent of Bowfell from the Wrynose Pass by the Crinkle Crags is the finest ridge walk in the District. On leaving the line of cairns keep to the crown of the moor for Cold Pike, to avoid bog as far as possible. From Cold Pike, crossing the moorland, look out on the right for a stream—it is the last running water on the route. The first Crinkle may be taken direct, but the second, and highest, presents a precipitous front—for people of experience only. By skirting the crags to the left for a short distance, a reasonable route to the summit may be found. The third Crinkle may be climbed or turned on the left according to fancy, but we would recommend the remaining two and Shelter Crags be turned on the left. They are very rough in parts and take up a lot of time. All along the route from Cold Pike the views on either side are of a very high order. From Cold Pike the Duddon Valley is seen to great advantage and the general prospect is superb, but not equal to that from the loftier Crinkles, which in turn must yield the palm to Bowfell.

During the final ascent, look out carefully for the commencement of the descent by the Band. If started too high one may get involved in quite awkward ground. In any case the Band can be reached by contouring round from the Three Tarns.

Towards the end of the descent of the Band the ridge is crossed by a wall. The path down is to the right and just short of this.

To the west the Scafell group, with the Mickledore Chasm, is grandly seen, with Great Gable a little north of it, partially concealed behind Great End. Far away, over the western sea, we can distinguish the Isle of Man. To the north we look along Langstrath and Borrowdale to Grassmoor and the adjacent fells, with Saddleback and Skiddaw on the northern horizon. Between these we catch a glimpse of the Solway, with the Dumfriesshire hills beyond. On the other side of Langdale are the Langdale Pikes, somewhat dwarfed from our lofty position, and in the distance the long range of Helvellyn and Fairfield, with peeps of High Street. To the south the wild Crinkle Crags, affording the finest and roughest ridge walk in the District, lead the eye to the Coniston Fells, which fall into the plain embracing Esthwaite and Windermere.

Note.—Bowfell is not only very rough but very complicated. Those who wish to pursue the ridge-line towards Esk Hause can continue over Esk Pike, or, descending by Ewer Gap, may join the track from Rossett Ghyll to Esk Hause. The Three Tarns may be reached from Langdale by Stool End Farm and Hellghyll. As a descent in thick weather it is unthinkable.

6. Helvellyn

(*See Outline Guide* (*i*), p. 42, *and Ullswater Section*, p. 109)

An easy ascent is to walk as far as Grisedale Tarn (1,768 ft.), take the zigzag route up Dollywaggon Pike and along the ridge-line to the summit, descending to Wythburn or the head of Dunmail Raise. Easier still is it to take the bus to Wythburn and ascend from there. Most of a day should be allowed for Helvellyn.

7. Coniston and Wetherlam

(*See Outline Guide* (*l*), p. 44)

The **Old Man** is the easiest mountain of its height to ascend, albeit the start is not quite easy to find. Coniston should be left either by a lane to the right of the *Black Bull* or to the left of the *Sun*, and Church Beck followed as far as the bridge over the Falls (*see* p. 44). Then climb steadily up to the left. Unfortunately the whole of the eastern face of the Old Man is disfigured by quarries and mines, and, though this is the regular ascent, visitors with an eye for beauty are recommended to follow the Walna Scar route for a short distance past Boo Tarn and then turn up the fell to the right, keeping to the ridge-line. On the other hand this route misses the beautifully-situated Low Water and the delicious spring above it, the one and only drink to be had on the whole round. In this case the final pull up is steep.

The prospect from the summit cairn is very extensive, and one of the most pleasing in the district. It is in a sense unique, on account of the sea view it commands. The mountain panorama is also very fine. To the east are the familiar peaks that start with the Helvellyn Dodds and terminate in Ill Bell. Ingleborough, with its flat top, is seen far off, and in the remote distance, more to the south-west, are the mountains of Snowdonia. At one's feet is Coniston Water, and then come Morecambe Bay, the Duddon Sands and Black Combe. The little tarn to the west is Devoke Water, 766 feet above sea-level, and farther off is the Isle of Man. Facing us as we turn is the splendid precipice of Dow Crags. Next the giants of the Scafell Group stand up magnificently and away to the north Skiddaw and Saddleback form a noble horizon.

From the cairn the route follows the ridge-line north, over delightful turf for the most part, with slight ups and downs. At the first depression, Levers Hause, the route may be joined by pedestrians from the Duddon Valley by turning left at the head of Walna Scar and following the ridge over Brown Pike and Dow Crags. Levers Water lies below us on the right and soon Seathwaite Tarn appears on the left, and so we tramp over How Crags to the summit of Swirl How, only five feet lower than the Old Man. The look-back here along the ridge is very striking. From this point a digression of about an hour there and back may be made to Grey Friar, which dominates the Duddon Valley. It is worth it. The return is made by Carrs, from which either the head of Wrynose or Little Langdale may be reached by the long ridge of Wet Side Edge and Rough Crags. The views of Bowfell during this descent are unsurpassed. Returning to Swirl How we drop steeply down to Swirl Hause. This descent is broken up by rock outcrops, but no difficulty need be experienced if they are passed on the right. From the Hause the route at first curves upward to the left and then goes on to Wetherlam, to reach which another depression must be crossed.

The prospect from Wetherlam has been much neglected. There are few finer, particularly to the North and round to the South-East. Also no fewer than fourteen lakes and tarns are visible from the summit: Red Tarn (Pike o' Blisco), Stickle Tarn, Blea Tarn (Little Langdale), Little Langdale Tarn, Elterwater, Loughrigg Tarn, Windermere, Blelham Tarn, Tarn Hows, Arnside Tarn, Esthwaite Water, Coniston Lake, Blawith Tarn, Low Water. The prospect during the descent is constantly delightful.

Note.—If descending from Wetherlam for Greenburn Bottom and Little Langdale, drop down left immediately on reaching the *col* and do not diverge to the right. Otherwise there is a risk of getting entangled in acres of unspeakable juniper scrub. The slopes of Wetherlam need special care on account of numerous disused mine-shafts.

The Northern (Keswick) Section

KESWICK

Access.—By rail *via* Penrith and by bus (*see* p. 8). For Road Routes *see* p. 9.
Angling.—*See* p. 16.
Banks.—*Midland; National Westminster; Lloyds; Barclays.*
Bathing.—The bathing place is at north end of Lake, west of the road to Friar's Crag. Open 7 to sunset.
Boating.—On the lake. *See* p. 17.
Bowls.—In Fitz Park.
Buses.—Regular services in summer to Borrowdale and Seatoller; Grasmere, Ambleside and Windermere; Bassenthwaite and Cockermouth; Penrith, Lorton, Ullswater; Buttermere; etc.
Car Parking.—Market Place (Saturdays excepted), Bell Close, Station Road, off Main Street, and in Lake Side.
Cinema.—*Alhambra*, St. John's Street (nightly).
Century Theatre, Dancing.
Early Closing.—Wednesdays.
Golf.—Putting and Miniature Golf Course, Lake Road, and in Fitz Park.
Hotels.—*Keswick; Derwentwater; Royal Oak; Queen's; Lake; King's Arms; Burleigh Mead; Chaucer; County; George; Harney Peak; Red House; Swinside Inn; Lodore*, Borrowdale, 3 m.; *Armathwait Hall*, Bassenthwaite.
Launches.—Launches make frequent trips up and down the Lake. Piers at the landings near Friar's Crag, Ashness, Lodore and Brandelhow Park.
Library and Reading Room, St. John Street: County Library.
Museum, Low Fitz Park, Station Road.
Places of Worship.—*Parish Church* (Crosthwaite), *St. John's Church, Congregational, Methodist, Roman Catholic*, etc.
Pony Trekking.—Walpole Hotel. Lakeland Trekking Stables, Troutbeck, Penrith.
Population.—4,500.
Post Office.—Main Street, near the lower end of the Market Place.
Tennis.—Hard and grass courts in Fitz Park. Annual Tournament in June.
Youth Hostels.—Keswick Hostel, Station Road. Derwentwater Hostel, 2 miles.

Keswick is a fairly large and prosperous market town on the banks of the river *Greta*, close to the northern shore of Derwentwater, perhaps the most picturesque sheet of water in England. It is the best centre in Cumberland for excursions through Lakeland. The town is very accessible, being connected with the L.M.R. main line at Penrith (18 miles) and having good bus services to and from many parts of the country.

In the centre of the main street is the **Moot Hall**, erected in 1813. The bell, brought from the Radcliffes' ancestral seat that formerly stood on Lord's Island in Derwentwater, bears the number 1001 (a mistake for 1601) and the letters H.D.R.O. The Radcliffes were Earls of Derwentwater, but forfeited their property after the Rebellion of 1715. The **Parish Church,** at Crosthwaite, a mile from the town, is dedicated to St. Kentigern (the "St. Mungo" of Glasgow). Near the east end of the south aisle is a white marble effigy of *Southey,* whose tomb is in the churchyard. The inscription on the monument was written by Wordsworth. The baptistery forms a memorial of *Canon and Mrs. Rawnsley,* whose work for the preservation of the beauties of the Lake District will never be forgotten. Among other features note the ancient font (1390), and the pitch pipe and baton with which singing was regulated in pre-organ days.

The **School of Industrial Art,** near the bridge on the Crosthwaite road, is worth a visit. Here also are the neat *Pencil Works.* The well-stocked **Public Library** is situated in St. John Street, near **St. John's Church,** the spire of which figures in every view of the town. The churchyard is worth visiting for the sake of the view of Derwentwater, seen in all its loveliness, from the terrace. It also includes the burial-place of Sir Hugh Walpole, the novelist.

A great annual event in Keswick is the *Evangelical Convention,* which takes place early in July and lasts a week; it was founded in 1875 by Canon Battersby, for many years vicar of St. John's, Keswick. Casual visitors are warned that during the Convention accommodation is invariably fully booked. Various sheep-dog trials are held in the vicinity.

Among the most attractive features of Keswick are the **High** and **Low Fitz Parks,** on the north bank of the Greta. Football, cricket, tennis and bowls are well provided for. At the gate of the Low Park is a **Museum and Art Gallery** (*fee*), containing Flintoft's model of the Lake District and, among other objects of interest, a fine stone organ, and many original manuscripts, including the original of the famous Cumbrian hunting song, *John Peel*; also letters of Wordsworth, Walpole and Southey. There are also some interesting collections of paintings including some single works by Turner, Girtin and Ruskin.

Greta Hall, the home of S. T. Coleridge for several years from 1800 and of Robert Southey from 1803 to 1843, stands on a low hill at the northern extremity of the town, a few hundred yards to the right of the bridge that crosses the Greta on the Crosthwaite road. The house forms part of Keswick School and is not shown to the public. Shelley, too, when obliged to quit Oxford, came to Keswick with his first wife, Harriet, and lived for a while at Chestnut Hill.

At one time the town was noted for its woollen manufacture, but now the chief manufacture is cedar wood articles, especially pencils. The mineral blacklead (plumbago) of which they are manufactured was formerly found in the mines at Seathwaite, in Borrowdale.

From Keswick, from Portinscale and from Borrowdale Valley, the facilities for walks and excursions are numerous. The Lodore Hotel, at the back of which are the celebrated Falls, is three miles from Keswick, and the Borrowdale Valley is 5 miles. Portinscale is a mile west of Keswick. For Road Routes *see* pp. 46–52.

WALKS FROM KESWICK

1. Round Derwentwater

There are two ways of starting this walk: (*a*) by taking the Borrowdale road (leaving St. John's Church on the left) and continuing past Castlehead, (*b*) by leaving the Borrowdale road at the Lake Hotel and turning to the right down Lake Road for Friar's Crag. The miniature golf course is passed on the right and, shortly beyond, the road continues past the boat-landings and along another footpath to **Friar's Crag.** This rocky promontory, about a mile from Keswick, is generally supposed to be so called because it was the landing-place of the friars of Grange. Others maintain that the name is derived from its being the wharf of St. Herbert, who in the seventh century lived on the island since named after him. On the crag is the **Ruskin Monument,** erected in 1900, a simple block of Borrowdale stone.

From the Crag nearly the whole of the Lake is visible. After much rain, the waters of Lodore, at the other end of the Lake, may not only be seen but heard from this point. From Friar's Crag walk back to a wicket-gate on the east side, and follow a path skirting the shore of the bay, at the far end of which enter Ings Woods by another wicket-gate. A well-defined path leads through the wood and over a bridge across the Brockle Beck. On the far side of the wood disregard the lane leading to the left and keep on towards Stable Hills. Go through the wicket here, and then through the wicket immediately on the right and cross a meadow to the lakeside, opposite Lord's Island. Hence keep along the shore of the lake as far as a spinney on **Broomhill Point,** a headland similar to Friar's Crag, and a fine view-point. From the spinney continue to follow the shore of the lake to Calf Close Bay. The remainder of the walk is through Great Wood, with **Walla Crag** (1,234 ft.) towering above on the left, to be succeeded by **Falcon Crag** as we emerge on to the Borrowdale road. A deep cleft in the face of Walla Crag, visible from the road, bears the name of the **Lady's Rake,** from the tradition that the Countess of Derwentwater made her escape from Lord's Island up the ravine on receiving news of the approach of the parliamentarians during the Civil War. Disregarding the lane leading up to Watendlath, we continue to follow the main road through the trees past Barrow House and Falls.

Three miles from Keswick, the **Falls of Lodore** (small fee for entrance) are reached by a path just beyond the *Lodore Hotel.* The "lion" here is, of course, the cataract, a lion which, except after heavy rain, roars as gently as any sucking dove. The ravine, however, is very beautiful. The upper falls should be visited. The stream falls through a chasm between the towering perpendicular rocks of Gowder Crag and Shepherd's Crag. These cliffs are draped with oak, ash, and birch trees, which impend from rocks at points where growth would seem impossible. In calm weather, an extremely fine echo is to be heard.

A mile or more south of Lodore is the village of **Grange,** with a double bridge over the Derwent, immediately on the other side of which is a large slab of rock bearing distinct glacial markings. Practically the whole of Borrowdale was given to the monks of Furness by Alice de Rumeli in 1209. Grange was the place where they stored their grain and also the salt made at the salt springs of which there were several near the village.

Crossing the Derwent by Grange Bridge, and turning northward, we reach the hamlet of **Manesty,** with National Trust woods near by. Proceeding at a considerable height along the open side of **Catbells** (1,482 ft.) we obtain one of the best views of the lake and valley, with Skiddaw and Saddleback in the background. The retrospect here is also very attractive. Below are the disused Brandelhow Mines, and, next to them in charming contrast, **Brandelhow Park.** From the north end of Catbells a pretty footpath near an iron kissing gate takes us across a road, through a wood, a meadow and another wood to **Portinscale,** about twenty minutes walk from Keswick. (Hotels at Portinscale: *Derwentwater*, *Harney Peak.*)

This walk round Derwentwater is about twelve miles, but in dry weather the distance may be reduced by about two miles, if a footpath is taken across the head of the lake from near Lodore to near Brandelhow. After much rain this is impracticable.

2. Castlehead

This, like Friar's Crag and Cockshott Wood, is the property of the National Trust and is only half a mile out of the town on the Borrowdale Road.

For the geologist Castlehead (or Castlet) is interesting as being all that is left of a volcano, to the eruptions of which the formation of the Lake District is primarily traced. To both geologist and tourist, Castlehead is also interesting as being the best view-point close to Keswick. The prospect from the summit (529 ft.) is very charming and extensive. At our feet is the Lake, dotted with richly wooded islets, among them **St. Herbert's Island, Lord's Island, Derwent Island** and **Ramp's Holme.** On the first-named lived St. Herbert, a disciple of St. Cuthbert of Holy Island. So attached were the two friends that they died on the same day, in accordance with the prayer of the hermit of Derwentwater. There is also in the south-east corner of the Lake, near Lodore, a **Floating Island.** It is generally submerged, but occasionally rises to the surface for a short time. This phenomenon is caused by the permeation of the sunken mass by marsh-gas during hot weather, the upward motion being assisted by growth of buoyant water-plants on its surface. On piercing the soil with a boat-hook, there is a strong escape of gas.

3. To Walla Crag

Follow the Ambleside road (bus service) until, a little beyond the Old Toll Gate, a road to the right leads to Rake Foot. Crossing a bridge, we walk over the open moor by a wall till we reach a stile which takes us to the top of **Walla Crag,** commanding a grand view of Derwentwater, Skiddaw and the Newlands and Borrowdale Fells. From the Crag the tourist may descend Cat Ghyll into the Borrowdale road where it passes through the Great Wood about a mile and a half from Keswick, or he may continue his walk by going over Falcon Crag and then down to Ashness Bridge.

4. To Watendlath

A ramble through this secluded valley is a pleasing addition to the ordinary walk round Derwentwater. It runs parallel with Borrowdale on the east. Though possible for cars, the road rises 600 feet in about $1\frac{1}{4}$ miles, and is fairly narrow, with few passing-places for vehicles. The stream which "comes down" the waterfall of Lodore issues from a beautiful little circular tarn in this upland valley. The road to Watendlath turns out of that from Keswick to Borrowdale beyond Walla Crag, and passes behind Barrow House, crossing a mountain stream over which is the picturesque *Ashness Bridge.* In the second wood beyond Ashness Bridge two paths, about fifty yards apart, are cut to the edge of the cliffs above Lodore. The view from either point is very dramatic, with almost a sheer drop to the lake many feet below. On leaving this wood, a path to the right leads down to the **Upper Lodore Falls,** which are worth visiting, both for themselves and for the fine views over Derwentwater. Going straight on, just before reaching Watendlath a gate to the right leads us to the **Churn,** a curious "punchbowl" with a hole in its bottom, which the Watendlath Beck has hollowed in the rock. At **Watendlath,** two miles from Lodore, a pretty bridge is thrown across the stream which issues from the tarn above. Refreshments can be obtained at the two farmhouses in the hamlet.

Leaving the tarn on the left, we follow a track over the fells for Rosthwaite. At first the surroundings are somewhat monotonous, till all at once, with the suddenness characteristic of the Lake District, a splendid panorama opens before us. Glaramara is in the middle distance, and beyond are the passes and peaks of the wildest part of Lakeland. The track descends rather steeply into the valley and, crossing a stone bridge, emerges on to the Borrowdale road close to the Post Office at Rosthwaite. The walk to Rosthwaite by Watendlath, returning by the road, is about thirteen miles. (For Rosthwaite to Grange, *see* Walk 6; for Grange to Keswick, Walk 1.)

5. To Grange Fell

Grange Fell, the great buttress which overlooks the entrance to Borrowdale from the east, was purchased by the National Trust in 1910 partly as a memorial of King Edward VII. The summit was accordingly christened the King's How. Access to the fell is indicated by notice boards on the roadside between Grange and Rosthwaite and a narrow path leads up the north face of the fell. It must be remembered that the fell is somewhat rough and the ascent is not quite such a simple grass promenade as Latrigg.

The view from the summit is superb. North are Derwentwater and the adjacent fells; south, at one's very feet, is Borrowdale, with a noble background of the highest and most rugged mountains in England. Away to the east are the Helvellyn and Fairfield ranges.

The descent must be made either by returning the same way or by a path which winds down in a southerly direction and meets the Borrowdale road between the Bowder Stone and Rosthwaite. Owing to precipitous crags it is impossible to get down direct to the west.

6. To the Bowder Stone and Rosthwaite

The Bowder Stone is near the Borrowdale Road and is situated on the lower slopes of Grange fell (*see* above, Walk 5.)

A mile from Grange Bridge and immediately beyond a large slate quarry is the famous **Bowder Stone,** a remarkable rock of prodigious bulk, which lies like a ship upon its keel. It is sixty-two feet long and thirty-six high; circumference, eighty-nine feet; weight, 1,970 tons. It is of rock alien to the local volcanic rock and was probably carried down by glaciers from Scotland; but that it should have come to rest in its present position is surprising. The stone is wonderfully balanced. From this point a fine view of the upper part of Borrowdale is obtained. A little beyond the Bowder Stone, on the opposite side of the gorge of Borrowdale, is a conspicuous rock eminence, called **Castle Crag,** the site of a British hill-fort. The view from the summit is a delight. Unfortunately the base of the Crag is rather difficult of access, but see the variation walk below. Overlooking Castle Crag is the bulky mass of Gate Crag, but the pick of the scenery during this walk is to be found in the famous "Borrowdale Birches" on the banks of the Derwent and the ever-changing mountain prospect in front. Borrowdale is the most beautiful valley in England, perhaps in Great Britain.

Variation. Cross Grange Bridge and turn to the left through the village and along a track which runs through the woods below Gate Crag. It is possible to follow the river nearly all the way to Rosthwaite, but the path is sometimes rather a scramble and the easier course is to keep to the track till Castle Crag is passed on the left, and then take a clearly-marked path down the slopes to Rosthwaite when that village comes into sight. This delightful walk is far preferable on a hot day to the main road, with its heavy traffic. Instead of descending through the woods to Rosthwaite, one may continue to follow the upland path, which eventually leads out on the Honister Toll Road with Seatoller at one's feet.

7. To the Castlerigg Stone Circle

Follow the Penrith road for about a mile and then, a hundred yards or so beyond the Ambleside turning, take a lane which goes off on the right. This is the old road to Penrith. The **Circle** is in a field immediately beyond Castle Lane, the first turning on the right. There are 48 stones remaining in the great circle, the tallest of them about 5 feet high. Within the eastern arc of the circle is a kind of sanctuary marked with additional stones. The origin of the circle is unknown, but was probably a meeting-place in the Bronze Age. If so, it is very much older than the time of the Druids, and it may be 3,000 years old. The situation appears to have been most carefully selected. From no equally accessible position in the neighbourhood can the visitor obtain the same commanding and magnificent view. He finds himself on an eminence in the centre of an immense circle of mountains, and obtains a panoramic view nearly a hundred miles in circumference, including a grand view of Saddleback, Skiddaw, Helvellyn, Grisedale Pike, and many other of the highest mountains of Cumberland, as well as of some beautiful vales.

The return may be varied by passing up Castle Lane to the Ambleside road; where turn right; or take the lane opposite, leading to Rakefoot and the routes outlined in Walk 1, Variation 1.

Or the excursion may be extended by following the old Penrith road and the next road (right) into the Vale of St. John, returning *via* St. John's-in-the-Vale Church.

8. To the Vale of St. John, Threlkeld and Brundholme Woods

This ramble permits of numerous variations by any of the side-paths between the Ambleside road and the Vale of St. John. It can, of course, be taken the reverse way, but this is not advisable, as it leaves a stiff bit of climbing for the end of the walk. The total length of the round is about twelve miles. The walk may be shortened some four miles by taking bus from Keswick to Smeathwaite and some five miles by taking bus or train from Threlkeld to Keswick.

The Ambleside road is followed to Smeathwaite Bridge, a mile short of **Thirlspot** (*King's Head*). During the steep ascent from Keswick the views to the right over Derwentwater and Borrowdale, and backward down the Vale of Keswick and Bassenthwaite, would demand halt and retrospect, even on a level road. The descent into Naddle commands the Helvellyn range and the basin in which Thirlmere reposes. After crossing the bridge at Shoulthwaite a look-out behind should be kept on Skiddaw, as at one point its summit, which is invisible from Keswick, comes into view.

From Smeathwaite the direction is due north, with the Helvellyn range on the right. Overlooking the meeting-point of the two roads is the celebrated **Castle Rock,** which from some points presents every appearance of a fortified castle, with towers, battlements and keep. It is well to look back two or three times after passing it. Some distance farther on is **Bram Crag,** fissured by one of the deepest gullies in the district, and next come the picturesque **Wanthwaite Crags.** During the greater part of this portion of the walk Saddleback is seen at its best, straight in front.

Three miles down the Vale is **Threlkeld.** Follow the main road towards Keswick for a few hundred yards, and then take the turning on the right. This road must be kept to, as it is particularly easy for strangers, for some reason, to get astray here. Once in **Brundholme Woods** the way is clear.

9. Skiddaw Terrace

At the road-junction beyond Greta Bridge bear to the right and follow the Bassenthwaite road for about ¾ mile to the first turning on the right beyond the railway bridge. This turning leads to Ormathwaite and on by a "terrace" road past **Applethwaite** to Millbeck, and the intervening mile provides, according to Southey, the best general view of Derwentwater, and certainly the prospect goes far to justify his opinion. From Millbeck the main road can be regained, and a return made to Keswick. Length of walk about seven miles.

Variation. Combine with Latrigg (No. 11).

10. Portinscale, with Newlands or Braithwaite

Immediately beyond the bridge over the *Greta* on the Crosthwaite road, a path to the left leads across the fields to **Portinscale,** rejoining the main road close to a bridge over the Derwent, which receives the waters of the Greta almost immediately after leaving the Lake. To the right Skiddaw dominates the scene; in front are the Lorton Fells, but the finest prospect is away to the left. The Newlands Fells are seen to great advantage; to the left of them is the basin of Derwentwater, with Borrowdale beyond, terminating in the frowning buttress of Great End. The little point between it and Glaramara is not Hanging Knott (as local informants sometimes say), but Esk Pike (2,903 ft.). To the left of Glaramara is High Raise, with its flat summit, and farther round are the familiar woods and crags overlooking Derwentwater.

From Portinscale (¾ mile) the walk can be continued to **Braithwaite,** a little over a mile farther on, and a circular return made by the road running up Newlands from that village, either by Swinside, or Stair, or any of the by-lanes. A better walk, however, is to **Newlands.** About half a mile beyond Portinscale along the road to Swinside is the beginning of a path on the left which leads through pretty woods to the base of Catbells (signboard). With Catbells on the left, a green track leads along the base of the fell until some old mines are reached, from which a rough path runs down to the right to Little Town. Our route is now to the left, and then, immediately after crossing a bridge, to the right for the main road to Keswick. Length of walk about eleven miles.

11. Latrigg

(*See Outline Guide* (*a*), *Skiddaw p. 36*)

Following the side-track indicated on p. 36, a very few minutes take one to the summit. The view is one of the most beautiful in the District. The prospect is similar to that from Castlehead, but more extensive. Notable are the Helvellyn Range on the left front, and Pillar above and beyond the Buttermere Fells. There is an almost "aerial" view of Keswick, apparently just at one's feet.

LONGER EXCURSIONS FROM KESWICK

1. The Honister Round

The Buttermere Valley is largely protected by the National Trust.

The route as far as **Rosthwaite** is described under Walks 1 and 6, on pp. 88-9 and 91-2. Immediately beyond Rosthwaite a valley opens to the left, which divides on either side of **Eagle Crag,** a noble rock, into the valleys of **Langstrath** to the west and **Greenup** to the east, by which walkers may easily pass into Westmorland by Langdale or Grasmere. At the hamlet of **Seatoller** (*Seatoller House*) begins the road over **Honister Hause.** For the first mile or so it is a stiff climb, but all the way up the backward views are very fine. At the summit of the pass one has a fine view of the forbidding flanks of **Honister Crag,** one of the most remarkable in the Lake District. It is some 2,000 feet above sea-level, and for more than 1,000 feet is a steep descent at an alarming angle; the upper part is a sheer precipice. Much of this face is honeycombed with slate quarries, where the world-famed Honister green slate is obtained. The summit of the crag, from which there is a splendid view of neighbouring lakes and mountains, is, however, easily reached from Honister Hause, but the descent to Buttermere over Fleetwith requires care, the ridge-line being closely followed. On the right as we descend the road towards Buttermere is **Yew Crag,** and soon Melbreak and Hen Comb come into view ahead between the walls of the pass.

Buttermere

This gem of the Lakes has a noble setting of mountains. Brandreth, Green Gable, Haystack, High Crag, High Stile and Red Pike form the background from the village, whilst Buttermere Moss and Robinson close in the view to the north. Fleetwith, Honister Crag and Dalehead, at the head of the Lake, seem to shut out all communication to the south-east. At its outlet the Lake is separated from Crummock Water by meadows and luxuriant woods and hedgerows, the background being dominated by Melbreak. There are both trout and char in Buttermere, and fishing tickets and licences (both of which are needed) can be bought in the village from a local representative of the National Trust.

Skirting the edge of the Lake, we pass below the picturesque gorge of Gaitsgill and reach **Buttermere** village. (*Hotels:*

Bridge; Fish; Hassness (Ramblers' Association); *Buttermere Youth Hostel. Buses to Keswick and Cockermouth.*) The best short excursion from Buttermere is to **Scale Force,** the loftiest fall in the district. The stream leaps, in one clear fall of nearly a hundred feet, between perpendicular walls of syenite, but the amount of water is only considerable just after heavy rain.

Take footpath to the left of Fish Hotel in Buttermere for about 200 yards, turn off through gate on right proceeding down the fields to Scale Bridge. Cross bridge, turn right on to Scale Force path and continue until the force is reached.

Crummock Water

is passed if the previous path to Scale Force is followed. If time permits, it is well worth while to walk farther along the edge of the lake to **Ling Crag,** a little rock promontory at the foot of Melbreak, for the sake of the view. To the right are the Buttermere Fells, with Honister Crag in the distance and Warnscale Bottom between. In front, the sharp peak is Whiteless Pike, with Rannerdale Knotts below, and the massive red bulk of Grassmoor on our left. Tickets to fish on Crummock can be had from the National Trust's representative at Buttermere or from their estate foreman at Loweswater who lives not far from the Scale Hill Hotel. A small charge is made. Boats can be hired (without boatman) from the National Trust at the Bridge Hotel.

From Buttermere the shortest way to Keswick (8 miles) is by **Buttermere Hause,** starting near the church. About 100 yards along the road Great Gable and Kirkfell come into sight for a minute over the Haystacks. At the top of the Hause, Robinson frowns on us on the right. The sensation at this point is the steep descent which begins immediately the first corner is turned. (*Cyclists,* dismount! *Motorists,* crawl!) The valley we are now entering is **Keskadale,** and the scenery, though comparatively tame, is attractive. The mountain in the distance in front is Saddleback. Presently Newlands Valley and Little Dale open finely on the right and Eel Crags present an imposing precipice. The remainder of the route is rather winding, through pleasant wooded

In Borrowdale (*H. A. Summers*)

Ullswater (*H. A. Summers*)

Distant Skiddaw, from near Keswick (*Valentine*)

Patterdale (*H. A. Summers*)

country, by Swinside and Portinscale to Crosthwaite and Keswick.

2. Round Thirlmere

The route as far as **Thirlspot** is described under Walk 8, p. 93. Thence the road runs along the side of **Thirlmere,** below the slopes of Helvellyn.

Thirlmere

Is now the chief source of Manchester's water supply, with which city, ninety-five miles distant, it is connected by a series of huge aqueducts. The lake is over three and a half miles long and about half a mile wide. The surface level has been raised fifty feet by means of a huge dam, eight hundred feet long and about a hundred feet high, across the foot of the lake. The dam is divided in the centre by a rocky knoll, which forms a natural buttress.

Thirlmere by itself having proved insufficient to meet all Manchester's water needs, this supply has been supplemented by Haweswater, another reservoir created by enlarging a natural lake. (*See* p. 152.)

Two miles from Thirlspot we pass the Straining Well of the Waterworks, designed to look like a castle and, a little farther on, reach—

Wythburn

eight and a quarter miles from Ambleside.

"Wythburn's modest house of prayer" derives most of its importance from the fact that Wordsworth wrote about it, but with its rough-hewn roof timbers, beyond which the bare slates are visible, and with its thick walls and deep-set windows, it strikes a note that one misses in many more pretentious buildings. Opposite the Church is the famous old Nag's Head Inn, now no longer inhabited.

The return should be made by the road along the western shore. Half a mile south of Wythburn, turn to the right. Near here one has a full-length view of the Lake; but a better view-point is a rock, with seats, between the road and the shore a mile or so northward. This western road passes below two forbidding crags, **Fisher Crag** and **Raven Crag.**

At the far end of the lake a roadway, sixteen feet in breadth, traverses the dam, connecting the western and the eastern roads, which also join some distance farther on.

3. Keswick to Windermere, by Thirlmere, Grasmere and Ambleside

Described in Route 2, as far as **Wythburn,** whence a mile and a quarter takes us to **Dunmail Raise,** for which, and the remainder of the route, *see* pp. 68 and 47–8. The eastern road by Thirlmere should be taken, otherwise Wythburn is missed.

4. Round Bassenthwaite Lake

Buses make the circuit of the Lake daily; the Cockermouth buses go along the west side and the east side alternately.

Hotels.—*Armathwaite Hall; Castle Inn; Pheasant; Swan.*

The delightful **Vale of Keswick** stretches from the head of Derwentwater to the foot of Bassenthwaite Lake. The route from Keswick lies through Portinscale and past **Braithwaite,** at the foot of the Whinlatter Pass. Passing through **Thornthwaite** the road skirts the base of **Lord's Seat** (1,811 ft.) and **Barf,** with its **Bishop,** a curious rock about half-way up the fellside, not unlike a man in a surplice. From time to time his Lordship is touched up with whitewash lest he should be unfrocked by the weather. Beyond Barf the road undulates pleasantly through a State Forest on the western margin of the lake to **Peel Wyke** (*Pheasant Hotel*). At this end of the lake we see for the first time the twin summit, the "double front," of **Skiddaw.** A little beyond, the road turns off on the right at the guide-post to **Ouse Bridge,** which crosses the Derwent as that river leaves the lake. Here, and at **Armathwaite** (*Armathwaite Hall*, with its extensive grounds, is now an hotel) close by, are the best views for those who keep the road generally pursued in making the circuit of the lake; but walkers may be able to make use of lanes and tracks nearer the edge of the water. The return is by Mirehouse, at the foot of the slopes of Skiddaw.

5. The Whinlatter Pass and the Vale of Lorton

The Whinlatter Pass is the least difficult route between Keswick and Crummock and Buttermere. The scenery at the western end is more pastoral than mountainous, but neither type of scene suffers by comparison.

To Portinscale as already described, but on approaching Braithwaite disregard the main road to the right (to Cockermouth) and keep straight ahead through the village. The way rises steeply, with good views across to Skiddaw, and on reaching the summit of **Whinlatter Pass** is 1,043 feet above sea-level. Vast numbers of young trees have been planted by the Forestry Commission hereabouts, and in a few years the slopes of Grisedale Pike, on the left, will be invisible from the road. From the summit the descent is long and continuous to the hamlet of **High Lorton,** where we turn sharply to the left and run through the beautiful Vale of Lorton to Crummock Water and Buttermere. Keswick may be regained by the same road, by Buttermere Hause, oı by Honister.

6. To Caldbeck and Threlkeld

This makes a fair motor round from Keswick. It presents a somewhat sombre back view of the Lake District, but the interest of John Peel is a powerful magnet, and the first and last parts of the route are very interesting.

The first six miles from Keswick are along the Carlisle road as far as the *Castle Inn* cross-roads where the Caldbeck road turns off to the right. After about a mile there are extensive views, and from the Hause (to the right again) Bassenthwaite looks specially fine, set in its basin of hills. The road continues by Uldale and through bare moorland country to—

Caldbeck

The village is chiefly of interest through its association with **John Peel,** the renowned huntsman, whose gravestone is to be seen in the churchyard.

"D'ye ken John Peel?" the famous Cumberland hunting-song, is known and sung in every quarter of the globe, but so few people know its history

that a few notes here may be of interest. Despite the common notion—arising from the erroneous alteration of the original in the latter editions—it was not "at Troutbeck once on a day," but at Caldbeck, in Cumberland, that John Peel was born and buried. His coat was grey (not "gay," as in the song) being homespun of wool from the local Herdwick sheep.

Here, at Greenrigg Farm, "back o' Skidda'," was the home of the immortal huntsman. His appearance was striking, for he stood six feet high and more, and with a form and gait quite surprising; "terble lang in th' leg and lish (nimble), w' a fine girt neb (nose), and gray eyes that could see for iver." The sport was a passion with him, and for it, we are told, he would at any time neglect any serious business or household cares. He passed to "the happy hunting fields" in 1854, aged 78.

John Woodcock Graves, the woollen weaver of Caldbeck, stated that he composed the words of the song in 1832, whilst he was sitting by the fire with John; and that the tune which inspired their rhythm was an old rant called "Bonnie Annie," which was being sung at the time by an old woman as she crooned to sleep one of Graves' own children. To the choirmaster of Carlisle Cathedral (Mr. Metcalf) is due the setting of this old melody.

The Fells (Keswick Section)

1. Eel Crag, with Dalehead, Hindscarth, Robinson, etc.

(*See Outline Guide* (*g*), p. 41)

A splendid circular walk of about thirteen miles. It is pleasantest first to row to Hause End or take the motor-launch to Brandelhow for Catbells and thence follow the ridge-line as directed; otherwise the best approach is the walk through the woods beginning half a mile south of Portinscale along the Swinside road. As we climb Catbells the view quickly expands. To the east is the Helvellyn range, and just over the north shoulder of Helvellyn itself a sharp cone is seen. This is Catchedicam. The view down, first into Borrowdale on the left, and Newlands on the right, from the Eel Crags ridge-line, and afterwards from Dalehead into Honister Pass and the Buttermere Valley, is both beautiful and impressive. From Dalehead cairn the prospect southward is grand. The noble peak to the left is Bowfell; next comes the Scafell group, with Great Gable and the Pillar, and close at hand are the craggy scarps of the Buttermere Fells. The view down Newlands is very striking. Buttermere, Crummock Water, and Loweswater come into view during this walk. Turning home on Robinson the Grassmoor Fells are on the left, but they are not seen to the best advantage. In descending, aim for Newlands Church.

2. Glaramara (from Rosthwaite)

(*See Outline Guide* (*e*), p. 38)

This is a grand mountain, very massive, and as a view-point almost equal to High Raise (*see* p. 82). The latter has the advantage, inasmuch as Glaramara can be seen from it, whereas the aspect of High Raise from Glaramara is decidedly tame. On the other hand, the view down Borrowdale from Glaramara is superior. It must be admitted, however, that except in a few places Glaramara provides a rather exasperating walk—rocks, heather, swamp nearly all the way, and the descent is not easy to hit off, especially in bad weather. In such conditions it is a fell that should be avoided; there is no more confusing summit in the whole Lake District, and its rugged "tors" are proverbial. In any case, during the ascent, note any landmarks which may be helpful in getting off. The buses between Keswick and Rosthwaite will be found convenient.

3. Grassmoor, with Grisedale Pike, Eel Crag, Causey Pike, etc. (from Braithwaite)

See Outline Guide (*b*), p. 37)

Grassmoor by the Force Crag (Coledale Pass) route is the easiest mountain to ascend from Keswick, and one of the finest view-points in the Lakes. From the cairns on its wide summit one can look right down on Buttermere, Crummock and Loweswater, and the Scafell group are seen almost at their best. They present an even finer appearance, however, from Wandhope and Whiteless Pike. From Wandhope there is a striking panorama of the Newlands groups.

There is a fine expedition over Grisedale Pike, on to Grassmoor, returning over Eel Crag and Causey Pike. Or, if the day is young, a descent may be made by Whiteless Pike (steep) to Buttermere, whence a return may be made by bus. If returning by Force Crag, the instructions to descend with Force Crag on the left are important. There is a misleading path towards the Grisedale Pike side of the crag which may lead to serious trouble. In ascending by Force Crag, be particular to note the return route. In any case, however, the crag may be turned by taking to the grass slopes on the right of the descent.

4. Helvellyn

(*See Ullswater Section and Outline Guide* (*i*), p. 42)

It is best to ride from Keswick to Wythburn and ascend from there. The descent can be made either by Helvellyn Ghyll or Thirlspot, or the mountain can be crossed to Patterdale in time to catch bus or boat. (Care is required in getting off the main mountain on to either Swirrel or Striding Edge.) A charming round is to reach Patterdale by Penrith and Pooley Bridge (bus), and Ullswater (boat), and cross Helvellyn to Wythburn or Thirlspot, taking one of the Windermere-Keswick buses on the return journey.

5. High Raise

(*See Windermere Section and Outline Guide* (*h*), pp. 82 and 41)

Ride to Rosthwaite, go back a hundred yards, cross the bridge, and take the path on the other side of the stream, behind the hotel, up Greenup till Lining Crag is reached. The path lies up the near side of the crag. But for the bad walking up the valley over loose stones and moraine heaps, this would be an easier expedition than Grassmoor.

6. Lord's Seat and Barf

The ascent is made from Thornthwaite. Skiddaw is seen at its best from this point. The Pike of Stickle, like a giant's thimble, is visible in a southerly direction.

7. Saddleback (from Threlkeld)

(*See Outline Guide* (*a*), p. 36)

Saddleback commands a magnificent view. Away to the east is the Crossfell range. Right in front is the Helvellyn range, with the Matterdale fells on the east; and on the west St. John's Vale and Thirlmere, with the Coniston fells beyond. Farther to the right is the Scafell Group, with Great Gable, and nearer the familiar fells round Derwentwater. Skiddaw shuts in the prospect to the west. To the north is the dreary Skiddaw Forest, with the Solway and the Scottish hills beyond. The distinctive feature of the mountain, however, is its imposing southern front, well seen from the high road between Threlkeld and Scales, or looking down from the ridge of the mountain.

8. Skiddaw

(*See Outline Guide* (*a*), p. 36)

Generally speaking, the higher one goes up a fell, the better the view. The prospect from Skiddaw comprises somewhere about four-fifths of the fells in the District, of course including those visible from Castlehead and Latrigg. Nevertheless, as the panorama gains in extent it loses in beauty. The view from the Low Man is superior to that from the High Man, and so on down the scale, through Lonscale Fell and Latrigg to the Dodd, which, as it takes in Bassenthwaite, is, to our mind, the best of all. It may be remembered that the fell that appears beyond High Stile is the Pillar Mountain. The Old Man at Coniston is easily recognised by its conspicuous cairn. To the west is the Isle of Man, and to the north are the Solway and Scotland. On a very clear day the hills round Moffat may be discerned to the north, while Criffel in Kirkcudbrightshire is a commonplace.

The Buttermere Fells

(*See Outline Guide* (*c*), p. 37; *also Ennerdale*, p. 120)

It is very well worth staying a day at Buttermere for the sake of traversing these fells. The expedition should be made from Scale Force and the ridge-line followed over Red Pike, High Stile and High Crag to Scarf Gap, returning by Gatesgarth. Strong walkers may, however, continue over the labyrinth of the Haystacks (*avoid altogether in misty weather*) and, sweeping round the head of Warnscale Bottom, descend over Fleetwith to Honister Hause. The scenery is very fine throughout. If time is limited, **Red Pike** should be unhesitatingly selected. The tourist will do well to face north first, then turn west, then south. At his feet is Buttermere, with the Newlands fells above it; beyond is Derwentwater, and Saddleback and Skiddaw close the horizon. Then come the Grassmoor Fells, falling steeply to Crummock Water, with Whiteside beyond. Between Crummock and Loweswater Melbreak stands up. Next Ennerdale Water appears, lying in the wild valley of that name, on the other side of which rises the grand front of Pillar Mountain. The Scafell group is also well seen. High Stile shuts out most of the view to the east, the distant mountains seen in that direction being the Helvellyn range from Fairfield to its northern extremity.

The Eastern (Ullswater) Section

PATTERDALE

Access.—To Penrith by the L.M.R. line and thence by bus to Pooley Bridge and boat up Ullswater. There are also direct bus services from Penrith to Patterdale and Brothers' Water. For **Road Routes** *see* p. 9.

Bank (Glenridding).—*Barclays* (Friday).

Boats.—*See* Introduction. *Launches* at boat-landing.

Distances.—*By road:* Brackenrigg Hotel, 6½ m.; Pooley Bridge, 8½ m.; Penrith, 14 m.; Troutbeck (Cumberland), 8½ m.; Ambleside, 9½ m.; Troutbeck (Windermere), 10 m.; Windermere, 14 m.; Bowness, 15 m.; Grasmere (pony-track), 9 m. (road), 15 m.

Hotels.—*Brothers' Water; Bridge House,* Glenridding; *Ullswater; Glenridding; Patterdale; Howtown; Brackenrigg.*

Places of Worship.—*Parish Church, Methodist Chapel* (Glenridding), *Friends' Meeting House.*

Population.—700.

Postal Addresses.—Patterdale, *via* Penrith; Glenridding *via* Penrith.

Post Offices.—Patterdale and Glenridding.

Pier at Glenridding. Regular services o motor yachts up and down the lake.

Patterdale, including Glenridding, is the principal centre for the Ullswater district. It is delightfully situated at the head of Ullswater and seems to nestle among the wooded slopes of the spurs of Helvellyn and St. Sunday Crag. Patterdale means, or is said to mean, Patrickdale and the place was "no doubt" visited by the Irish saint: the church is dedicated to him, and there is a well near the village where he used to baptise converts.

In 1927 and again more recently Keppel Cove Tarn, situated three miles from the lake, 1,350 feet up, between Catchedicam and Raise, tore out a gap in the dam at its foot, and seven million cubic feet of water were precipitated down the fellside with serious consequences, but after the second occurrence the dam was not rebuilt.

Much of the land surrounding the head of the lake is protected by restrictive covenants with the National Trust.

Popularly the interest of **Patterdale** is confined to the voyage up Ullswater, the ascent of Helvellyn, and, incidentally, a visit to Aira Force. Its circumscribed situation, shut off seemingly from the central portions of the Lake District by a lofty barrier of mountains has led many to overlook the possibilities of Patterdale as an excursion centre. The list on p. 107 shows how mistaken is this notion. Of the favourite central resorts Windermere is accessible *via* the Kirkstone Pass and the beautiful Troutbeck Valley, and Keswick may be more easily, if less pleasantly, reached by bus (*summer, two per day*).

ULLSWATER

Boat Service.—There is an excellent service of boats up and down the lake between Pooley Bridge and Glenridding in the summer, calling at Howtown on the way.

From Pooley Bridge there is a regular service of buses to and from Penrith, for the L.M.R. main line and the branch to Keswick.

Hotels.—At Pooley Bridge: *Crown; Sun.* *See also* p. 104.

Ullswater, smaller than Windermere but larger than any other English lake, lies amid majestic mountains. It is of irregular figure, roughly resembling the letter Z, and composed of three unequal reaches. The shortest is seen from the Ullswater Hotel, and is not half the length of the others. The total length is over seven miles; the breadth varies from half a mile to close on a mile; the depth is 205 feet, ranking after Windermere (219 ft.) and Wastwater (258 ft.). It combines a great variety of attractions, portions of its banks possessing the sylvan beauty of Windermere, while the mountain masses at its head are scarcely inferior to those of Wastwater.

Wordsworth wrote: "In order to see the lower part of the lake to advantage, it is necessary to go round by Pooley Bridge, and to ride at least three miles along the Westmorland side of the water, towards Martindale. The views, especially if you ascend from the road into the fields, are magnificent."

The voyage up the lake occupies about an hour. The conical wood-clad hill close to the pier at Pooley Bridge is **Dun Mallet**, which commands an excellent view up the lake and across to Helvellyn. This is the site of a British hillfort. *Caerthanock*, close at hand, may also be a British fort, but it is not of the hill type.

On the east shore is **Barton Fell,** and behind it **Moor Divock** (1,061 ft.), an extensive plateau on which are several ancient cairns and stone circles. A low hill between Barton Fell and the lake was, according to a local antiquary, the site of "the ancient and noble fortification called **Trestermont,** or Tristermount," the abode of Sir Tristram, one of the Knights of the Round Table.

The boat next calls at **Howtown** (*Howtown Hotel*), the nearest point for pedestrians visiting High Street and Haweswater. To the west attention is attracted by the wooded slopes of **Hallin Fell** (1,271 ft.), on the summit of which is a monument to Lord Brougham. A stone seat on the south of the cairn commands a magnificent prospect of the hills and lake. Near the fell is a precipitous crag, jutting into the lake, and crowned by a few stunted bushes. It is known as the **Kail Pot,** on account of a round hole in its face, just above the edge of the water. A zigzag road up the fell leads from Howtown to **Martindale Church,** about a thousand feet above sea-level, one of the loneliest churches in Britain.

Leaving Howtown, we see, on the opposite shore and looking up the middle reach of the lake, **Hallsteads**, situated on **Skelly Nab,** the point which juts out into the lake at the commencement of the second reach. From this point to Geordie Crag, opposite, old-time fishermen used to stretch the gwyniad (or skelly) nets, capturing these fishes by the cartload. The rest of the voyage is beautiful in the extreme. The bulky mass of **Place Fell** (2,154 ft.) shuts out the view to the left, but in front and to the right are richly-wooded shores leading up into lovely dales, whilst over all frowns Helvellyn, an imposing background. The pointed cone somewhat to the north of the almost level summit is Catchedicam; and a little to the south a sharp peak marks the end of Striding Edge.

Silver Point, immediately below Place Fell, is the division between the second and third reaches of the lake, **Glencoyne,** with its park and fell, marking the change of direction on the other bank. In this glen are some cottages, very properly named *Seldom Seen*; and the little stream running through it divides the counties of Westmorland and Cumberland. **Stybarrow Dodd** (2,756 ft.) forms the background, and **Stybarrow Crag** the foreground of the picture.

Away to the left, **St. Sunday Crag,** *the* Ullswater mountain, presents a noble front. Some distance beyond its foot we can trace the commencement of Kirkstone Pass, flanked to the west by Red Screes and to the east by Caudale Moor.

Walks from Patterdale

1. To Aira Force and Gowbarrow (6 miles).
2. Grisedale Tarn and back (8 miles).
3. Ascent of Helvellyn by Glenridding Valley, returning by Grisedale (13 miles).
4. Ascent of High Street; drive to Brothers' Water, thence walk (14 miles in all).
5. To Mardale over High Street.
6. To Howtown, *via* Boardale Hause (a diversion to Angle Tarn is recommended) (12 miles return).
7. To Grasmere, *via* Grisedale Tarn (9 miles).

The beautiful valley of **Glenridding** is, alas, defaced by a large lead mine; but there remain Glencoyne, Grisedale, Deepdale, Dovedale, the Pasture Beck Valley, Hayeswater Ghyll, leading up from Low Hartsop, and beyond, from the lakeside near Sandwick and Howtown, Boardale, Bannerdale, Ramps Gill and Fusedale. With regard to the walks up these dales we can but repeat the advice given, under the Windermere Section, viz. to ramble up the valley as far as one feels inclined, and to ramble back by the way one likes best. We shall confine ourselves to one of these glen walks—Grisedale Tarn—not because the others are inferior in beauty or interest, though Grisedale is, in the opinion of competent judges, the finest of the Ullswater valleys, but because it forms part of a popular pass for walkers between Ullswater and Grasmere.

Aira Force and Gowbarrow Park

Gowbarrow Fell and Aira Force, now happily in the care of the National Trust, make a lovely tract of some 750 acres affording glorious views of Ullswater and the surrounding fells, whilst now and again, if fortunate, one may come on a herd of red or fallow deer. The route from the village lies along the Lakeside as far as the Matterdale turning (say 2¼ miles from Glenridding) whence the path is clearly marked; on the way one may leave the road and go through the lovely **Glencoyne Wood** (National Trust), and there is also a pleasant footpath, avoiding the main road, through Glencoyne Park.

Between the road and the Lake, half a mile from Glenridding, is **Stybarrow Crag**, an attractive little cliff bedecked with trees. It was here that one of the Mounseys, of Patterdale Hall, obtained the title "King of Patterdale" for his gallantry in repulsing, with the aid of a few villagers, an invasion of Scottish moss-troopers.

The approach to **Aira Force** and the surroundings, woodland and park, are delightful. The force itself makes a leap of some sixty feet sheer between precipitous walls of rock, and when in full volume is really impressive. Below and above, bridges span the gorge, adding to or detracting from—according to the taste of the visitor—the picturesqueness of the ravine, but in any case making it easy of access. There is an abundance of footpaths in every direction.

Nearer the lake is **Lyulph's Tower,** an eighteenth-century shooting-box of the Howard family. The reputed origin of Lyulph is Ulf, or L'Ulf, a former Baron of Greystoke, who would seem to have bequeathed his name to Ullswater.

Grisedale Tarn

S ee also Windermere Section, p. 67)

From the pier the road for Patterdale village should be followed. After passing the grounds of Patterdale Hall turn sharp to the right up **Grisedale**. From Patterdale it is the first turning to the left beyond the Church. The main stream should be kept on the right for about two miles till it is crossed a little below Eagle Crag. The fine mountain on the left is St. Sunday Crag, a dependency of Fairfield which overlooks the head of the Pass. Almost in front are the precipices of Eagle Crag, with Dollywaggon Pike beyond and on the right are, first, the rounded, wooded spurs of Striding Edge, then the grand declivity of the Edge itself. From Grisedale Tarn (1,768 ft. above sea-level)—wind, vigour and weather permitting—the return may be made over St. Sunday Crag, descending to Elmhow (*see* p. 110). It is well to remember, however, that it is a stiff slant from the foot of the tarn up to Deepdale Hause, and that St. Sunday Crag is a mountain to be respected.

Three other very fine walks from Patterdale are—

1. To take the boat to Howtown and return by the margin of the lake, or rounding **Hallin Fell** and reaching the lake shore again at Sandwick. From this point the mass of Helvellyn forms an impressive background to a charming prospect of lake and woodland.

2. To take the boat to Howtown and return, diverging to the left a little beyond Martindale Church, by Bannerdale or by the next valley on the left, up **Boardale**, and so over Boardale Hause (1,260 ft.). The mountain background from the summit of the hause is superb, and at our feet is all the loveliness of Patterdale.

It is not recommended these routes be taken the reverse way. Walking thus, one turns one's back on the finest of the scenery. On the boat it is easy to look over the stern. Indeed, in our opinion, the many changing beauties of the head of Ullswater are better seen on the voyage down the lake than when approaching from Pooley Bridge.

One can, however, of course walk out from Patterdale as far as Sandwick or Howtown instead of taking the boat, returning by Boardale Hause, and this route has much to commend it. The entire round is not much over twelve miles.

3. To Haweswater from Hartsop or from Howtown. The route from Hartsop passes close to Hayeswater and crosses the ridge to the north of the summit of High Street, after which it is best to aim for Kidsty Pike

and then descend into Riggindale. There are several routes from Howtown over the Martindale fells to Haweswater, and we recommend descending by the Measand Beck, which reaches the lake 1½ miles from the dam at the outlet. This can be made into a day's round by using the ramblers' path (see p. 110).

Longer Excursions from Patterdale

1. To Windermere by Kirkstone Pass and the Vale of Troutbeck (Westmorland), returning by Ambleside over Kirkstone Pass (30 miles).
2. To Grasmere by Troutbeck (Westmorland), returning as in Drive 1 (33 miles). Or on foot over Grisedale Pass.
3. To Gowbarrow and Watermillock, returning by Matterdale Hause and Dockray (16 miles).
4. To Lowther Castle by Pooley Bridge and Askham (27 miles).
5. To Haweswater by Pooley Bridge and Lowther Castle (45 miles).
6. To Keswick by Matterdale, Threlkeld and Castlerigg Stone Circle (32 miles).

Several of these may be made by bus or coach.

The Fells (Ullswater Section)

Helvellyn

(*See Outline Guide* (*i*), p. 42)

The popular vote is for Helvellyn. No able-bodied person who goes to the Lakes seems to be content unless he has made the ascent, so that we feel bound to devote somewhat more space to this mountain than to others whose merit, in our opinion, is greater. Helvellyn, in return for the compliment, proves himself the most accommodating of fells.

The ascents from Keswick, Grasmere and Ambleside have been indicated elsewhere (*see* pp. 101 and 84 respectively).

From **Patterdale** the routes of ascent are:

By the pony track, ascending by Glenridding and the Lead Mines round Keppel Cove Tarn (1,825 ft.); or from Grisedale Tarn (1,768 ft.) and over Dollywaggon Pike—a rather long round. Or by either Swirrel or Striding Edge. The path on Striding Edge is narrow, between two precipices, but there is no danger whatever for anyone who can walk steadily. The descent from Helvellyn to Striding Edge is down nasty steep scree and broken rocks, but the worst part of the ridge is its reputation. In any case and anywhere, should the tourist feel giddy, it is better to rest, or, failing that, to go back. There is nothing more to be ashamed of in giddiness than in seasickness. Swirrel Edge also requires care, and there is one quite awkward little bit near the upper end. The most noteworthy feature, however, is Catchedicam, which presents perhaps the finest front in the district.

Helvellyn is supposed to have been the sacred hill of the early inhabitants of the District. Some believe it to have been originally the Hill of Baal, or El-Velin, so Helvellyn.

Readers of Scott and Wordsworth will remember the poems recalling the fatal accident which happened to Mr. Gough, when attempting in winter-time to cross the mountain. The faithful dog watched by his master's body for three months until the remains were discovered. The late Canon Rawnsley laboured to establish the traditional story of the dog, and in 1890 he and Miss Frances Power Cobbe erected a monument to the memory of that animal "in order to mark the spot where the accident occurred." The memorial is a useful guide, particularly in bad weather, for it is some 50 yards above the "walk-off" for Striding Edge.

A monument commemorating an achievement of another kind is the cairn a short distance below the summit on the south side, with the inscription:

The first aeroplane to land on a mountain in Great Britain did so on this spot on Dec. 22nd, 1926. Bert Hinkler and John Leeming on an Avro-Alpha landed here and after a short stay flew back to Woodford.

The **View from Helvellyn** is very extensive. Facing east, at our feet is Red Tarn, flanked by Striding and Swirrel Edges. Beyond is a portion of Ullswater and on the horizon are the Pennine fells, with Cross Fell in the centre. Turning north, to the left, the masses of Saddleback and Skiddaw close the prospect. To the left of these, over Bassenthwaite Lake, appears the Solway, with the Dumfriesshire hills beyond. Then come Grassmoor and the Newlands fells. The graceful peak of Grisedale Pike may serve as a guide. Almost due west is Honister Pass. Next the Pillar stands out boldly, and a little farther down the head of Great Gable is unmistakable. South of this the Scafells assert their pre-eminence. Still turning, the shapely peak of Bowfell gives another landmark, from which Crinkle Crags lead the eye to the Coniston Fells, falling steeply to Coniston Water. The conspicuous points between us and Crinkle Crags are the Langdale Pikes, and beyond them is Black Combe. In the open space to the left of Coniston are Windermere and Esthwaite Water. Facing nearly south, Fairfield and Red Screes block the view. To the left is the cone of Ill Bell, from which the long level High Street range trends eastward.

St. Sunday Crag

(*See Outline Guide* (*i*), p. 42)

The ascent should be made by following the path to Grisedale Tarn, with the rivulet on the right till just beyond Elmhow, and by a beck running down from St. Sunday Crag, a track goes zigzagging up the fellside. This leads to a depression from which a brief ascent to the right takes us to the summit of the crag. The view comprises the best portions of Ullswater at our feet. To the left and right as we face west, are the precipices of Fairfield and the Helvellyn range, and, away beyond, the long line of fells that run from Scafell Pike by the Bowfell range to Coniston. In fine weather the walk may be pleasantly, if carefully, extended over Cofa Pike to Fairfield, from which a descent may be made to Grisedale Tarn.

Place Fell

Place Fell is as pleasant an afternoon ramble as any in the neighbourhood of Ullswater. The summit is most easily reached from Boardale Hause, striking to the left up the fellside. Place Fell commands delightful near views of the glens that adorn the head of Ullswater. Helvellyn is seen at its best, and Fairfield stands up grandly. Away to the north are Saddleback and Skiddaw. From the summit Howtown may be reached by dropping down diagonally into Boardale, or a return may be made to Patterdale by following the ridge-line towards Hallin Fell. When the slope steepens, by keeping down to the left in the direction of Scalehow Beck, a broad grass track will be found which joins the lakeside route between Patterdale and Howtown close to Sandwick. Care must be taken to start with Scalehow Beck, left, as the ground beyond is very rough and steep.

High Street

See Outline Guide (*k*), p. 43)

From Gatescarthfoot at the head of Haweswater (p. 152) the easiest ascent of the High Street range is by Kidsty Pike. The path along the west side of the lake is followed as far as the Riggindale Beck. Following the channel upwards for a short distance, we cross another, *Randale Beck*, by a foot-bridge. From this point our course lies upwards to the right, occasionally over somewhat broken ground, which is best negotiated by keeping a little to the right.

A more sporting route is by Rough Crag, the ridge-line of which should be reached as easily as possible. The path goes fairly directly up the tongue of land embracing Rough Crag and starting from High Street. A little short of the juncture of the ridge with High Street, Blea Water is seen below on the left, gloomy and impressive. It can be visited from the ridge, which can easily be regained. Or following the Nan Bield path (that to the right at the head of Mardale and the termination of the new road) to beyond Small Water, and nearly to the ridge, a depression to the right takes one to High Street, from which the line is north-west across easy grass to the top.

From the summits of the High Street range fine views are obtained in the direction of the Eden Valley and the Pennines. Towards the inner Lake District—westwards—the prospect is alluring; we want to see more of what is beyond. Saddleback and Skiddaw stand up finely to the north; Helvellyn and Harter Fell show to advantage; the eastern side of the Ill Bell range falls towards Kentmere with striking abruptness. Still we have a bit of Windermere here, a *peep* of the Buttermere Fells there, and so forth. It is well worth while to follow the summit line southward to Thornthwaite Crag (*see* p. 80), easily distinguishable by its columnar cairn. Any extra exertion will be more than compensated by the view. From Thornthwaite Crag a return can be made to Mardale by the Nan Bield Pass.

Harter Fell

(*See Outline Guide* (*k*), p. 43)

Harter Fell dominates the head of Haweswater. From the termination of the new road, follow the Gatescarth Pass till the summit is reached and before the path commences to drop towards Long Sleddale, turn to the right and bear west. A short distance below the summit a cairn marks an exquisite view-point down on to Haweswater. From the summit itself a wonderful panorama opens to the south-west from the Coniston fells round to the Fairfield range, which blocks the view to the north-west. The Mickledore Gap between Scafell and Scafell Pike is especially well seen. To the right of the spurs of Helvellyn is Saddleback. The return is made by Nan Bield, care being taken not to stray to the left, and then down by Smallwater to Gatescarthfoot. The Haweswater Hotel is two miles down the road towards the other end of the lake.

Little Langdale, from Wrynose Pass (*J. Hardman*)

Hardknott Pass (*J. Hardman*)

Wastwater, and Great Gable (*J. Hardman*)

Honister Pass (*J. Hardman*)

The Western Section

Eskdale—Wasdale—Ennerdale

Of this wild and beautiful region a great part is accessible only to the walker. Though there is no regular bus service into Eskdale, the Ravenglass and Eskdale Railway provides a useful service. Of recent years bus services from some of the principal Lakeland centres and from outlying towns have opened up the beauties of other parts of this district to those for whom the passes are too severe. It remains, however, and happily, a preserve in the main for the walker.

The Western District comprises:

1. Eskdale, with Bowfell, Crinkle Crags, and the fells that bound the valley to the west and south.
2. Wasdale, with the Screes, Scafell, Scafell Pike, Great Gable, Kirkfell and Red Pike.
3. Ennerdale, with the Pillar Fell, Scoatfell, with Steeple, etc.

These mountains are more easily ascended from Wasdale, but they really belong to Ennerdale, which also has a strong claim on Great Gable.

Eskdale

The **Esk** rises on the higher slopes of Great End, and runs into the sea near Ravenglass, where with the *Irt* and *Mite* it widens into an estuary, the northern boundary of which is formed by Drigg Point.

Motorists approaching from the south leave the main road just short of the village of Holmrook, about three miles after passing **Muncaster Castle** (*see* p. 139). Coming from the north turn aside at Gosforth by the road through Santon Bridge to Eskdale Green.

Boot is a small but attractive village in the dale, and is a good place at which to spend a summer holiday, though accommodation must be secured well in advance. (Hotels in vicinity: *Bower House*; *Burnmoor Inn*; *Lutwidge Arms*; *Woolpack*.) The air is pure, and the village close to the grand scenery in and around Wastwater and Eskdale. Two good fishing rivers, the *Esk* and the *Mite*, flow through the neighbourhood, and the *Irt* and *Calder* are not too far away (*see* p. 16). Near the village is a pretty fall, the water tumbling over rocks for a considerable distance. The waterfall and the old corn-mill, with its overflow water-wheel, near the rustic stone bridge over the stream, are favourite subjects for artists. There are two other "forces" in the neighbourhood. One, **Birker Force,** on a beck of the same name, has its source in a small tarn on the western slope of **Birker Fell,** and, after a course of little over a mile, tumbles over the fell into the Esk about a mile south-east of Boot. The cataract in flood is one of the most noteworthy in the district, despite its tame setting.

Stanley Ghyll, or Dalegarth Force

A little to the west of Birker Force, is unquestionably the finest in this part of the country. It is romantically situated in a deep and thickly-wooded ravine, about half an hour's easy walk from Boot or 25 minutes from Dalegarth railway terminus. The road turns off on the left at the old village school and crosses the Esk near *Dalegarth Hall*, an interesting old place. It has been for centuries the property of the Stanley family. The stream issues from a deep cleft in a perpendicular rock and leaps at a bound into a pool forty-two feet beneath. There are in all four falls in the glen; from the last the water runs with great force along its narrow channel. The beck rises on the edge of **Birker Moor,** across which runs the direct road from Boot to Ulpha. From this road, a little above the fall, the view up Eskdale is very fine indeed. Those who trace the stream to the higher ground will be close to **Devoke Water,** a tarn more than half a mile long, and famous for its fine red trout. The lake is the feeder of a small tributary of the Esk, the *Lin Beck*, on which are some pretty cascades. A little to the south-west of the tarn, and near the bank of the river, are some ruins known as the city of **Barnscar.** Tradition has it that the "city" was a settlement of the Danes; that they "gathered for inhabitants the lads of Drigg and the lasses of Beckermet," two villages on the coast to the north of the Esk; and that thence arose a local proverb, "Let us go together like the lads of Drigg and the lasses of Beckermet."

EXCURSIONS FROM BOOT

Upper Eskdale

We follow the road for Hardknott Pass, past the *Woolpack Inn*, till, just before the ground commences to rise towards the pass, a lane to the left leads to Butterilket Farm which belongs to the Forestry Commissioners and is part of their "Hardknott National Forest Park." (Three adjoining farms, Taw House, Wha House and Penny Hill belong to the National Trust.) Turning our backs to the rocky summit of **Harter Fell** (2,140 ft.), which has been conspicuous on our right throughout the walk, we follow the left bank of the Esk. Bowfell appears in front, to the right are the scars of Hardknott and across the stream Heron Crag, and other outlying buttresses of Scafell, shut in the valley.

A well-marked track leads to **Esk Falls,** a pretty series of cascades. Here *Lingcove Beck* is crossed by a bridge, and the main stream channel followed into the upper valley 500 feet above. After about a mile, on rounding a spur of Yeastyrigg Crags, **Scafell Pike** (3,210 ft.) comes dramatically into view. It springs almost its entire height from the valley and looks a mountain, aye, every inch a mountain, and one of which Englishmen may be proud. All here is very wild and desolate. Across the valley Cam Spout Crag, a rugged spur of Scafell, shuts out the Mickledore Chasm. There is a fine waterfall (Cam Spout), which is worth visiting, and the energetic may climb to the top of the **Mickledore Ridge,** between Scafell and the Pike, for the sake of viewing the grand Scafell Crags, a long and heavy grind. The return from Cam Spout is made under the buttress of Scafell and Slight Side. There is not much trace of a path here at first, but the general principle is to keep high up, or avoid keeping low down, till Cowcove Beck is reached. Here descend to the left and make for Taw House Farm (*National Trust*).

Wastwater by Irton Fell, returning by Burnmoor

Follow a track from Eskdale Green into Miterdale and then take a good fell path over the lower hills that extend from the Screes. On crossing the ridge-line we have one of what may almost be called the "regulation" surprise views the Lake District constantly affords. **Wastwater** is below us, the foot of the lake charmingly wooded, the head overshadowed by stern, rugged mountains. A descent is made to **Strands** (*Hotel*), and thence by the lakeside (p. 117) to **Wasdale Head** (*Wastwater Hotel*). To return to Eskdale retrace your steps for ¾ mile along the road and turn left over two bridges. Immediately beyond the second, a turn left through a gap in the wall leads to an unmistakable track over the depression between Scafell and the Screes, past Burnmoor Tarn (852 ft.). Some recommend that this expedition should be taken the reverse way on account of the fine view of the Pillar range with Kirkfell; but Wastwater should be *first* approached from its foot, and the mountain prospect can be enjoyed without much loss by looking back during the ascent of the Burnmoor track.

Crinkle Crags and Bowfell

(*See Outline Guide* (*e*), p. 38)

The ascent of these mountains is fully described on p. 83, as a walk from Langdale. It is an equally good expedition from Eskdale, the usual procedure being to follow the Lingcove Beck upwards from the bridge (mentioned on p. 115) two miles from Butterilket Farm, and bear right-handed.

Harter Fell

(*See Outline Guide* (*e*), pp. 38-40)

Harter Fell has the distinction of being the one "true peak" of the District, the use of hands as well as feet being necessary to attain the summit. The best views are in the direction of the Scafell and Fairfield ranges. This mountain must not be confused with Harter Fell at Haweswater.

Ravenglass by Railway

Another popular excursion from Boot is to take the miniature railway to Ravenglass and back. The line runs down Eskdale to Eskdale Green, then crosses into Miterdale and follows the north side of Muncaster Fell to Ravenglass. It is an excellent way of seeing the countryside. The station at the Boot terminus is called Dalegarth and the intermediate stations are Beckfoot (for the Country-Wide Holidays Association's guest-house), Eskdale Green, Irton Road and Muncaster.

WASDALE*

Hotel.—*Strands,* Nether Wasdale.

The best approach to Wasdale is from the west—for vehicles there is no option—as those who come from this direction

* Sometimes spelt Wastdale, but Wasdale is correct. In its earliest known form 1294 even Wastwater had no "t" and was "Wassewater."

have the advantage of seeing the lake with a grand mountain background. The district is entered at the hamlet of **Strands.** Visitors will be well advised to explore **Hawl Ghyll,** at the lower end of the Screes, at any rate for a distance. It is singular and impressive and of real interest to the geologist.

Close to the foot of the ghyll, at the spot where the River *Irt* issues from the lake, the very finest view of Wastwater is obtainable.

The Screes extend the whole length of the southerly shore of the lake. The summits are bare crags, the sides crumbling débris of a slaty and granitic nature, "streaked with brilliant hues of red and brown, like the changing colours of a pigeon's neck." Here and there huge rocks, fallen from above, rest on slopes in such positions as to suggest that the slightest touch will send them into the lake, and, indeed, considerable rock-falls take place periodically. The track along the shore of the lake at the foot of the Screes is practicable, but not advisable, being excessively rough and boulder-strewn.

As we approach **Wasdale Head** the scenery increases in sternness and grandeur. In front are the Scafell masses, the gully-seamed Pikes' Crag, a little below and on our side of the summit cairn, standing up prominently. To our left, overlooking the Sty, is **Great Gable,** one of the most perfect mountain forms in England, with Kirkfell next, and then the ridge of Yewbarrow, looking like a sharp pike, with a rough face towards the lake. Wasdale Head itself is full of reminiscences of Will Ritson, a great character and former landlord of the inn. Wasdale Head boasts the highest mountain, the deepest lake, and the smallest church in England, *i.e.* one of the several "smallest churches" in England. The church was built in the seventeenth century and its simplicity is entirely suited to its surroundings.

Wasdale Head is circumscribed by steep fellsides and intersected by stone walls. Nevertheless, some pleasant rambles may be taken, both along the road and up the side-valleys. Eskdale may also be visited (*see* p. 115). Boating is to be had on the lake, and the angler will find some sport. But first and foremost Wasdale Head is essentially a centre for hill-walkers and climbers.

Scafell Pike* and Scafell

(*See Outline Guide* (*e*), p. 38)

It is advisable to allow the greater part of a day for climbing either o these mountains, or a full day if the two are taken together.

From Wasdale route (*c*) (p. 39) by Brown Tongue is the easiest. It is important to remember that Pikes' Crag, the great riven bastion facing the ascent, must be left on the right. The aspect of Scafell precipice, farther to the right, is magnificent. A descent can be made over Broad Crag and Ill Crag to Esk Hause (the line of ascent from Langdale or Borrowdale), and so back to Wasdale by the Sty. On this last route, from whatever direction taken, two points must be remembered, that the last drinking-water on the route is the beck immediately behind Great End, and that the ascent of Great End for the sake of the view must not be omitted. The stretch of water which comes into view on the north-west on this route is part of Crummock.

From the Sty Head, in case of wild weather on the tops, the following route (the **Corridor**) may be taken. In the Great End Crags looking towards Wasdale is a conspicuous rift, Skew Gill. Make for this and a line of cairns will soon be picked up which leads along the base of the Pikes, past the heads of Greta Gill (care required) and Piers Gill, to the old wall in the depression between the Pike and Lingmell, close to which the Brown Tongue route is joined. But this Corridor route is better as a descent, because the best of the scenery is then before you. It should only be undertaken in clear weather. In the event of mist, hug the base of the crags, otherwise you may get mixed up with Piers Gill, which would be disastrous.

That part of Scafell Pike above the 3,000-feet contour was dedicated to the nation by Lord Leconfield as a tribute to the heroism of the men from the dales who fought in the Great War.

The summit of England is called Scafell Pike (3,210 ft.) for convenience. Formerly the tops of its buttresses were called "The Pikes" simply, and it is only comparatively recently that they have borrowed a name from their formidable neighbour. The name, therefore, means "The Pike near Scafell."

* In dissyllabic names in the Lake District the accent is generally on the first syllable, *e.g. Scaw*fle, *Skid*der, *Bow*ness; not *Scafell*, Skid*daw*, Bow*ness*.

Many tourists desire to pass from Scafell Pike to Scafell. Frankly we do not think it good enough. The northern and eastern faces are not to be thought of and though the northern face can be turned by a long, arduous and steep scree shoot, *Lord's Rake*, the enthusiasm of the individual must decide whether the reward is commensurate with the time and energy expended. No other route must be attempted. There have been too many fatal accidents on this mountain already.

View from Scafell Pike.—Southward in the immediate foreground is the magnificent Scafell precipice. Beyond is the Isle of Man and, far far away the Mourne Mountains in Ireland are occasionally visible. Turning due south, beyond the Duddon Sands and Black Combe, one may discern the Welsh Carnedds, and then, quite close, Bowfell with Crinkle Crags, and the Coniston Fells. Still turning to our left we catch a glimpse of Windermere. The flat-topped fell farther away is Ingleborough in Yorkshire, and the sharp cone nearer is Ill Bell. Eastward is the long Fairfield and Helvellyn range, with peeps of High Street and Kidsty Pike beyond; the mountain seen through the gap is St. Sunday Crag. Saddleback and Skiddaw and a strip of Derwentwater below are on the northern horizon. Immediately in front in this direction, Great Gable rises magnificently. The cone beyond is Grisedale Pike, with Grassmoor and the Buttermere fells nearer at hand. Next comes the Pillar Range, and next a bit of Wastwater.

Scafell is most easily ascended from Wasdale; or from the *Woolpack*, Eskdale, *via* Eel Tarn; or from Boot *via* Burnmoor, and a long weary grind it is, with heavy collar-work at the finish. For scenery, however, the Upper Eskdale route from the Eskdale side is incomparably finer, but also more arduous.

The **view from Scafell** is similar, except that the Pikes block out much of the prospect to the north. On the other hand, we can see Wastwater to much greater advantage.

From Scafell Pike the best return to Wasdale is by Great End and Sty Head or by the Corridor. The going over Broad Crag is rough, but the view from Great End of Great Gable, Derwentwater and Borrowdale will more than recompense the fatigue.

Great Gable

(*See Outline Guide (f)*, p. 40)

Failing the glorious ridge walk from Honister Hause over Brandreth and Green Gable, this beautiful mountain is best ascended either from the Sty Head, from which the ascent can be made direct, or from **Sty Head Tarn** (1,430 ft.) by Aaron Slack and Wind Gap between Great and Green Gables. In matter of time there is not much to choose, but the direct route is preferable, if steeper, on account of the views. The Aaron Slack route involves a long grind up a boulder-lined valley which effectually cuts off all views except those behind one. The descent is best made by Wind Gap.

The alternative and obvious route from Wasdale is up Gavel Neese, the southerly ridge, but the upper stages are very steep and intricate. Under mist the tourist might go seriously astray, and get into difficulties amongst crags.

The view from Great Gable is superb. To the south the Scafell group cuts off the distant scenery, but we can afford to sacrifice distance to such a splendid foreground. Bowfell stands up finely beyond Esk Pike. Away to the east, beyond Allen Crags and the High Raise fells, are the High Street, Fairfield and Helvellyn ranges. A little to the left of Bowfell we have a peep of Windermere, with the Yorkshire fells beyond. To the north the eye travels up Borrowdale to Saddleback and Skiddaw, and so round by Grisedale Pike to the Grassmoor fells. Near at hand are the Buttermere fells, with Robinson and the Newlands fells beyond. Under Grassmoor we can see Crummock Water. Next comes the wild and lonely valley of Ennerdale, and to our left the grand front of Pillar Mountain, with the Pillar Rock prominent below the summit of the main mass. Still farther to the left are Red Pike, Yewbarrow and Wastwater, flanked by the Screes.

On a boulder near the summit cairn, facing north, is the bronze **War Memorial** tablet of the Fell and Rock Climbing Club, engraved with a relief map of the neighbouring peaks, purchased by the Club and presented to the nation through the National Trust.

The Screes

(*See Outline Guide* (*e*), p. 38)

We recommend going up from the foot of Wastwater near Strands, and coming down to the Burnmoor track near Wasdale Head Hall, as it is preferable, if possible, to traverse the ridge-line from SW. to NE. for the sake of the grand background of mountains facing you. In addition the views down into the lake are very striking.

ENNERDALE

Ennerdale is more difficult of access than Wasdale, and is now even more exclusive owing to the Forestry Commission having taken over a large portion of the upper valley. The Scarth Gap–Black Sail path is untouched but the road from

Bowness Knotts (car park) to Scarth Gap is closed to cars. Gillerthwaite itself is in the possession of the Commission.

The chief driving excursions from the foot of Ennerdale Water are to Calder Abbey (*see* p. 140), Loweswater and Buttermere.

The walking is even more circumscribed than in Wasdale. Scale Force and Buttermere can be reached by Floutern Tarn (*see* p. 129), but the best plan is to row the length of the lake and wander up the valley. Alternatively there is a road of sorts as far as Gillerthwaite Farm (4 miles) or a path round the other side of the lake by Angling Crag (rather longer). The first of the great mountains is Steeple, with its wild crags, next to it the Pillar towers magnificently, then comes Kirk Fell, and at the head of the dale Great Gable looks superb. Between these two mountains Kirk Fell sends down some fine crags. The walking at the extreme head of the valley is vexatious, owing to the glacial mounds, and much of the ground above Gillerthwaite is fenced off for plantations forming one of the State Forests. It is worth bearing in mind that Ennerdale is a very long valley: from Gillerthwaite to the Youth Hostel, where the Scarth Gap–Black Sail route from Buttermere to Wasdale crosses the Liza, is four miles, and to Gable another two miles, making a total of ten from the foot of Ennerdale Water.

Pillar Mountain

(*See Outline Guide* (*d*), p. 38)

The **Pillar Rock** is on the north face of the fell. It was thought inaccessible until 1826, when an adventurous cooper succeeded in climbing it. If we are to believe Wordsworth's well-known lines from *The Brothers*, a previous ascent had been made with disastrous results. It is probable, however, that Wordsworth confused the rock with Ash Crag, nearer Black Sail Pass. Since 1826 the rock has been climbed repeatedly, but the ascent, even by the easiest route, is for cragsmen only. Many tourists wish, however, to see this famous rock. It is well viewed from Scarth Gap or the Gables and from Ennerdale itself, provided one does not get too close under the fellside. Those who wish to *visit* the rock may do so from the top of Pillar Mountain by a steep descent which requires great care, but a fairly reasonable approach is by the climbers' path from Looking Stead direct to the base of the rock.

From Wasdale or Buttermere **Pillar Mountain** is almost always ascended from Black Sail (*see* p. 128). Nevertheless, the ascent from Gillerthwaite, in Ennerdale, is to be recommended, if only for the fine views of the Steeple, a spur of Scoatfell. This mountain and the Wasdale Red Pike can be included in the Pillar Mountain expedition without undue fatigue, and very well worth a visit they are.

The view from Pillar Mountain has been much neglected. It is splendid. Right at our feet is Ennerdale, bounded by Great Gable to the east and the fine screes of the Buttermere Fells to the north. Beyond these are Robinson, Hindscarth and Dalehead, with Skiddaw and Saddleback in the distance. West of these is the great red mass of Grassmoor, with the adjacent fells. To the east, beyond Great Gable, is the Helvellyn range, and to the south we look down over dreary Mosedale, with the grand background of the Scafell group.

The Passes

Visitors to Lakeland who find mountain-walking too fatiguing and yet desire to escape from the high roads may find delightful recreation on the passes. At the same time those who are only acquainted with Honister, the Kirkstone, Buttermere Hause, Whinlatter, Dunmail Raise, and even Wrynose and Hardknott, are warned that for the most part the passes are not metalled roads, or even cart-tracks, but mountain paths, some of which are exceedingly rough and in places steep, *e.g.* the Sty, Coledale, and, worst of all, Rossett Ghyll.

Motorists will find notes on Honister, Whinlatter, Kirkstone, etc., on pp. 46–52, etc.

To Cyclists. Kirkstone Pass, Honister, Buttermere Hause, Whinlatter Pass and Dunmail Raise are all rideable. Special attention should, however, be paid to the advice given on p. 14. Hardknott and Wrynose are negotiable, but the gradients and corners are very bad. The descent from the Garburn towards Windermere could be ridden in parts. The others are *emphatically* not rideable. Many cyclists have carried their machines over Scarth Gap, and even the Sty and Esk Hause, but this "pass storming" is a thing apart.

Following is a list of the principal Passes, showing the manner in which they connect the four sections of Lakeland into which this Guide has, for convenience, been divided:

The Southern Section is connected with the *Northern Section* by Dunmail Raise (vehicular traffic), Far Easedale and Greenup, and the Stake; with the *Eastern Section* by the Kirkstone Pass (vehicular traffic); Grisedale Pass; Scandale Pass; Troutbeck, Thresthwaite Cove, and Pasture Beck; and the Nan Bield Pass, besides which the Garburn connects Troutbeck and Kentmere; with the *Western Section* by Wrynose and Hardknott (vehicular traffic, *see* above) for Eskdale, Walna Scar for the Duddon Valley, and Rossett Ghyll and Esk Hause by Sty Head for Wasdale.

The Northern Section is connected with the *Southern Section* by Dunmail Raise (vehicular traffic), Greenup and Far Easedale, and the Stake; with the *Eastern Section* by the Sticks (the Helvellyn range can be rounded by motor *via* Troutbeck and Matterdale); with the *Western Section* by the Sty, Scarth Gap and Black Sail, Esk Hause, and by the Floutern Tarn route.

Within the section are the Honister Pass (*see* p. 94), Buttermere Hause (*see* p. 96), the Whinlatter Pass and the Coledale Pass.

The Eastern Section is connected with the *Southern Section* by the Kirkstone Pass (vehicular traffic, *see* p. 78); Grisedale Pass; Scandale Pass; Pasture Beck, Thresthwaite Cove and Troutbeck; and the Nan Bield Pass; with Longsleddale by the Gatescarth Pass; and with the *Northern Section* by the Sticks Pass.

The Western Section is connected with the *Southern Section* by Walna Scar; by Hardknott and Wrynose (possible for vehicular traffic) from Eskdale; by the Sty, Esk Hause and Rossett Ghyll from Wasdale; with the *Northern Section* by the Sty, by Black Sail and Scarth Gap, and by the Floutern Tarn route.

Several of the more important passes, such as Dunmail Raise, Grisedale and Kirkstone Passes, are described elsewhere in connection with Drives or Walks from the various centres (*see* Index), and we need only here include the passes not so described.

Far Easedale and Greenup

From Grasmere strike off north-westward into **Far Easedale,** which runs far into the hills on the western side of Helm Crag. Up this seldom-visited valley, the walker can ascend laboriously to a wide, spongy tract of moor, after which he will cross Greenup Edge and drop down by Lining Crag and Greenup Gill, into the Stonethwaite branch of Borrowdale, and so northward to Keswick. Care must be taken to go by Far Easedale, not by Easedale—which is on the left soon after quitting the high road, and easily recognisable by a stream called *Sour Milk Ghyll*, flowing from Easedale Tarn—and not to turn down to the right into Wythburn after leaving Far Easedale.

Stake Pass

The **Stake Pass** from Langdale to Borrowdale starts from a sheep-fold two miles from the *Dungeon Ghyll Hotel* and climbs up to the right. The path to the left leads by Rossett Ghyll to Esk Hause, for Wasdale. Ascending the Stake, which is always exceedingly wet, the track zigzags up by the side of a stream, which dashes down into Langdale. Half a mile beyond the top of the Stake begins the descent into Borrowdale by the side of the beck, through the valley of **Langstrath.** Cross the stream by the first bridge, about a mile beyond where the valley bottom is reached, or by another bridge two miles farther on. On the right, not far above Bull Crag, is a large and curious stone, called **Blea Crag.*** Nearer Stonethwaite is the bold rocky elevation of **Eagle Crag,** on the right at the junction with the Greenup valley. From **Stonethwaite** the road to Keswick is by the village of **Rosthwaite** (*on bus route*) in Borrowdale. (Hotels at Rosthwaite include *Scawfell* and *Royal Oak.*)

Scandale Pass

For route as far as High Sweden Bridge, *see* p. 62. A mile and a half farther there is a sheep-fold, after which the path ascends the hill straight in front till a stone wall is reached. Crossing this in the direction of Red Screes we soon come to the descent into **Caiston Glen,** which leads down between Red Screes and High Hartsop Dodd to the Brotherswater Hotel. The stream should be crossed as high up as possible below the bog and the descent made with it on the left.

Troutbeck, Thresthwaite Mouth, and Pasture Beck

For **Troutbeck** *see* p. 59. Ascend with the beck on the right to Thresthwaite Mouth, the well-marked *col* between Thornthwaite Crag and Caudale Moor. It is well to rest at the top of the pass for the sake of the view. Behind are the Troutbeck Valley and Windermere; in front is the head of Ullswater, with fine crag scenery on the left. The commencement of the descent from the hause is very steep and then the Pasture Beck is followed downwards. The Windermere–Patterdale road is reached just below Brothers' Water. The expedition is a little fatiguing, but we recommend it in preference to the Kirkstone Pass.

The Nan Bield Pass from Windermere

Walkers may save some fatigue by taking bus or train to *Staveley*, but we recommend the inclusion of the **Garburn Pass,** for the sake of the views of Troutbeck Valley and the surrounding fells. The descent into Kentmere is fine, but the road up that valley to the

* This is the celebrated Gash Rock, reputed inaccessible by Colonel Barrow and named by him after a guide called Gash.

reservoir is only remarkable for the "close up" of Rainsborrow Crag. By turning to the right, passing the church with its yews, and turning to the left over the bridge, a parallel track is reached, which passes Overend, and, beyond Hollowbank Quarter, slants up the fell and over its shoulder to the Nan Bield Pass. This route is greatly to be preferred.

The head of the Nan Bield Pass is remarkably cleanly cut, and presents a really formidable outline. From the summit of the pass we have a striking view of the precipitous sides of Ill Bell and of Rainsborrow Crag. In front is the enlarged Haweswater, and at our feet Small Water. The track descends past this tarn and at Gatescarthfoot joins the track from Longsleddale (p. 129).

Wrynose and Hardknott

Many and ingenious attempts have been made to give the etymology of the singular name, Wrynose. The evidence of a twelfth-century entry, however, appears conclusive. The pass is there described as *Wraines-hals.* There may be some divergence of opinion as to the exact spelling, but there is none as to the general meaning—"the Pass of the Stallion," *i.e.* the pass which requires a strong horse—which it certainly does. Wrynose was part of the Roman Road from Ambleside to the coast *via* Hardknott.

At Fell Foot Farm at Little Langdale, a short distance beyond Little Langdale Tarn, we begin the ascent of Wrynose by one of the steepest roads in the district.

During the ascent Wetherlam, Swirl How, and Carrs are conspicuous on the left, overlooking a fine combe sparkling with cascades. The monotony of the descent is relieved by the fine outline of Harter Fell on the far side of the valley. Soon after crossing the Duddon at Cockley Beck a glimpse may be obtained of Scafell Pike and Ill Crag up Mosedale on the right. Almost immediately after we begin to ascend—

Hardknott

separating the head of the Duddon Valley from Eskdale. Though the road continues to be very bad, the scenery improves till we reach the summit, from which the charming **Eskdale** lies open, with its hamlets and sheep-farms, as far as the sea, whilst the Scafell mountains rise grandly on the right. To the north, within a hundred yards of the road rather more than half-way down are the ruins of **Hardknott Castle,** which was a Roman fort commanding the pass. There are remains of extensive buildings in the centre of the area, and at the four gates lie larger heaps of stones than at any other part of the walls, except at the four corners, where there is evidence of the existence of round towers. Between the fort and the road the ruins of the bath house are still quite visible.

Walna Scar

From Coniston pass under the railway bridge and after a stiff pull up continue across the open moorland with the Old Man on the right. A little short of Torver Beck a track to the right leads to Goats Water and Dow Crags, an hour's divergence well worth the making. The main track leads easily to the summit of the pass and so to a magnificent surprise view of the Scafell range and a charming prospect of the Duddon valley. It is well to remember that the Walna Scar track ends quite suddenly half a mile up the valley beyond Seathwaite Church and the Newfield Inn.

Rossett Ghyll, Esk Hause and the Sty Head

The track starts from the sheep-fold at the head of Langdale, two miles from the *Dungeon Ghyll Hotel.* It turns to the left—the path to the right leads to the Stake Pass—and soon the ascent of Rossett Ghyll commences. **Rossett Ghyll** is one of the few places in the Lake District we reach without satisfaction and quit without regret. It is very steep, and extremely rough, albeit these disabilities can be modified by a wide divergence towards Bowfell.

From the head of Rossett Ghyll the track leads through some of the wildest and sternest scenery in Lakeland. Soon we descend temporarily and pass on our left Angle Tarn, overshadowed by Hanging Knott, a shoulder of Bowfell.

On our right opens **Langstrath,** which is a regular trap in misty weather for walkers coming from the west. (Let these take warning that the head of Rossett Ghyll is beyond and not to the left of Angle Tarn.) Next we pass between Esk Pike on the left and Allen Crags on the right, reaching Esk Hause. (Left to Scafell Pike: right down Grain Ghyll to Borrowdale.) We proceed straight on below the grand precipice of Great End, with a fine view down Borrowdale to the right, with Skiddaw on the northern horizon above Derwentwater. Next we pass **Sprinkling Tarn,** at an altitude of 1,960 feet, and so reach the **Sty Head** (*see below*). The tarn to our right is **Sty Head Tarn** (1,430 ft.)—the path beside it leads to Stockley Bridge and Seathwaite in Borrowdale; in front Great Gable stands up grandly, its fantastic Napes Ridges well defined against the sky, and on our left is the majestic group of the Scafells, riven at their base by the wild ravine of Piers Ghyll. From this point the track descends westward steeply and roughly to Wasdale Head but Wastwater is for some time hidden behind Lingmell, an abutment of the Pikes.

The Sty

is known popularly and in maps as the Sty Head. The proper name of the pass is the Sty (vernacular, *stee,* ladder). The word appears to be related to the Norwegian *Sti,* a narrow foot-path. The Sty Head is simply the head of the Sty.

The route from Seatoller is *via* **Seathwaite,** which meteorologists say is the wettest inhabited place in England. From Seathwaite a track rises gradually to Stockley Bridge where it crosses the beck. The **Sty Head Pass** is now in front. At the head of the valley (Grain Ghyll) on the left, Great End is prominent; then comes the dip of Esk Hause, and behind is Glaramara. On the right of our track is a fine waterfall, **Taylor Ghyll Force.** After a stiff ascent of some 1,000 feet, an easy and well-marked, though occasionally wet, path leads past the **Sty Head Tarn,** a little short of the top of the pass.

For scenery and the descent to Wasdale, *see* p. 116.

The Sticks Pass

This is between Stanah, near Thirlspot (*see* p. 93), and Glenridding, by the Greenside Mines. The summit of the pass is marked by a series of sticks. Fine views, but given good weather we should always recommend tourists to cross Helvellyn by its summit in preference. The exertion is not much greater, and the scenery is incomparably finer.

Scarth Gap and Black Sail

Fine as is the route from Wasdale to Buttermere, it is well worth while to make this excursion in the reverse direction. The route starts from Gatesgarth, at the head of Buttermere, which lies in soft beauty on the right, whilst to the left is the rugged valley of Warnscale Bottom. During the ascent fine backward views are obtained to the north in the direction of Skiddaw. For a time the scenery becomes somewhat tame, then suddenly the head of Ennerdale comes into view with startling effect. All here is wild and lonely. To the right is the grand front of Pillar Mountain, with Pillar Rock standing out boldly. In front Kirkfell sends down some noble crags, and to the left is the majestic face of Great Gable. We descend into Ennerdale, cross a bridge almost opposite the Youth Hostel, and ascend **Black Sail**, with Kirkfell crags *on our left*. The bridge is the guide. It points directly to the foot of the Black Sail Pass, whereas the general trend of the path descending from Scarth Gap is thoroughly misleading. From the summit of Black Sail the path descends steeply amid grand and impressive scenery, Kirkfell on the left and Pillar, Red Pike, and Yewbarrow on the right, till, all at once, with dramatic suddenness the gaunt crags of Scafell spring into sight. Then the dale opens out displaying Wastwater, backed by the strange precipice of the Screes. Wasdale Head is quickly reached.

Esk Hause, by Grain Ghyll

From Keswick to Eskdale.

The route is first *via* Seatoller and Seathwaite to Stockley Bridge. After crossing the bridge, we turn left through a gap in a wall and follow the stream (*Grain Ghyll*), keeping it on our left for some time till the ground begins to rise steeply, when we cross and ascend by a tongue which protrudes into the valley. There is also a rough track on the other side of the beck. The mountain on our left is Glaramara; that on our right Seathwaite Fell. In front Great End is a grand object. At its foot we join the Sty Head path, and a short climb to the left brings us to **Esk Hause.** Here bear right, between Great End and Esk Pike, and in a few minutes we find ourselves looking down into Eskdale, with the crags of the Scafell Pikes on our right and a long shoulder of Bowfell sweeping down on the left. For **Eskdale,** *see* p. 113.

Floutern Tarn Route

Between Buttermere and Ennerdale.

This pass is frequently sloppy or worse; also it is disappointing. Crossing to the western district, one is always in expectation of being rewarded by a reputed grand view of Ennerdale, which, after all, is only partially realised and that at the very end of the walk. On the reverse route the branch track to **Lowes Water** affords pretty peeps, but we get at Buttermere all wrong, as the approach from this direction does not show the beauties of this most charming valley to advantage.

Coledale Pass

Between Braithwaite and Scale Hill.

The route as far as the head of the pass from Braithwaite is identical with that taken for the ascent of Grassmoor (p. 37). From this point the track descends roughly between Grassmoor and Whiteside amid wild, rugged scenery. To walkers we recommend this route in preference to that by the Whinlatter Pass (p. 99).

Gatescarth Pass

This leads from Longsleddale to Haweswater. The valley of Longsleddale, which starts at Garnett Bridge (4 miles from Kendal) makes a good approach to the district, as, after one has seen the pick of the beauties of Lakeland, its scenery loses by comparison. Nevertheless, the valley and the pass are well worth a visit. The head of Longsleddale is wild and rugged, but after this the walk takes us through featureless grass slopes. The chief interest here lies in keeping to the path. At the head of the pass it is important not to turn to the left on to Harter Fell, and to the right is the branch pass to Swindale and Shap; we keep on in a northerly (slightly north-westerly) direction. The descent, however, is delightful. To the right lies the enlarged Haweswater, with steep cliffs sloping down to its new shore line. In front is the High Street range, seen at its best, and to the left the craggy face of Harter Fell. The foot of the Pass is called Gatescarthfoot and this is at the terminus of the road made by the Manchester Corporation as part of their water-works scheme and as substitute for the old road now submerged by the reservoir. It is two miles down the road to the *Haweswater Hotel* (the only house in the Haweswater basin), four miles to the other end of the lake, and six miles to the village of Bampton.

The Coast Section

To Lakeland through the Furness District

Before dealing with the many places of great historic interest and natural beauty which lie between the mountains and the sea, a word or two must be said concerning the much-frequented seaside resort of—

Morecambe

Morecambe is often referred to as the "gateway" to the Lake District. The facilities for exploring the southern part of Lakeland by steamer, rail, coach and car are so excellent that many visitors make this resort their headquarters. Splendidly situated on the shores of spacious Morecambe Bay, it rivals Blackpool for its abundant provision for the amusement of visitors. In addition to the piers, with their pavilions, there are the Winter Gardens, four other theatres, four magnificent ballrooms and other places of entertainment. The promenade is six miles long. From almost any part of the sea-front a magnificent panorama of the Lakeland Fells expands along the opposite side of the Bay. From the Bare End (East) the prospect extends from Black Combe and the Old Man to the Howgill Fells and Ingleborough in Yorkshire. The facilities for bathing, boating and fishing are excellent. There are two good golf links, and the country around affords many delightful drives and rambles. Some of the most popular circular tours through Lakeland may be conveniently made in one day from Morecambe. In the neighbourhood too, are the historic city of **Lancaster,** with its famous castle and fine old parish church, and **Heysham,** with a church certainly not less interesting. In recent years a fine new road has been made along the shore northward, forming an admirable link with the London–Carlisle road (A6) at Bolton-le-Sands.

This, however, is a digression. Proceeding north-west from

Carnforth Junction, the distributing railway depot for tourists entering Lakeland from the south, we first reach—

Silverdale

Golf.—Nine-hole course.
Hotels.—*Silverdale; Royal.*

Silverdale is three and a half miles from Carnforth. The somewhat scattered village—nearly a mile west of the railway line—occupies a charming site on the eastern side of Morecambe Bay, more or less opposite Kent's Bank on the western shore.

Of recent years the channel of the River Kent has tended to move farther out from the shore leaving a wide expanse of grass land which is completely covered only by the highest tides. There is a fine open view towards the sea with particularly good sunsets.

Silverdale is fortunate in the wealth and variety of wild flowers which have made their home in this favoured bit of limestone country. Extensive areas of woodland, freely open to the public are owned by the National Trust and there is an abundance of attractive woodland and country walks.

Arnside

Hotels.—*Inglemere; Crown; Albion.*

Coach Excursions to Kirkby Lonsdale, Ingleton, Levens, Yealand, etc., and into the heart of Lakeland, including Derwentwater, Ullswater, Grasmere, Rydal and Windermere.

This, the only "port" on the brief coast of Westmorland, occupies a pleasing site on the east shore of the Kent estuary, opposite Grange, with which it is connected by a long railway viaduct, of fifty spans of thirty feet each. Boating is a great attraction, but swimmers should beware of the tidal bores. The growth of Arnside has not spoiled the charm of the coast or of **Arnside Knott** (National Trust) from the top of which one of the finest views in this part of the country is obtained. A little to the south of the knott is the ruined **Arnside Tower,** thirteenth century. It was much injured by fire, 1602. It appears to have been something of the nature of a Pele Tower on a large scale. There are similar erections at Beetham, Hazelslack and Wraysholme. Like the latter, Arnside Tower is connected with the legend of "The Last Wolf."

Arnside to Kendal

The main road skirting the east bank of the broad estuary of the Kent and Bela rivers (which join at Sandside) onwards to Milnthorpe, is nearly level, and is an excellent one when not flooded by tidal waters, which occasionally happens, as it is only a few feet above normal sea-level. From **Sandside** a road and foot-paths lead over Haverbrack Common to the **Fairy Steps,** formed by the action of water on the front of a lengthy perpendicular range of limestone. The Fairy Steps are a favourite resort of tourists and picnic parties from Morecambe and other places.

Beetham is prettily situated at the junction of the Silverdale road with the Lancaster-Kendal main road. The church is both pretty and ancient.

Heversham, a mile and a half north of Milnthorpe, has a fine old Church, rebuilt after a disastrous fire in 1601, but known to have existed in the eleventh century and perhaps as early as the eighth. The Grammar School was founded and endowed in 1613 by Edward Wilson.

The main Kendal road by-passes Heversham, a mile beyond is **Levens Hall.** with its famous clipped yews (*see* p. 145), and a further five miles northward we reach **Kendal,** described on pp. 142–44.

The road to the left at Levens Hall leads to Lindale and Grange-over-Sands, which looks across the Kent estuary to Arnside and Silverdale.

Grange-over-Sands

Bankst—*Barclays; National Westminster* and *Midland*.
Bathing Pool at west end of Promenade.
Bowls.—Public greens adjoining Promenade.
Early Closing.—Thursdays.
Excursions from Grange.—Cartmel Priory (3 m.); Humphrey Head (4 m.); Holker Hall (5 m.); Newby Bridge (7 m.); Lake Side, for Windermere (8 m.); Witherslack and Whitbarrow (7 m.); Levens Hall and Gardens (9 m.); Bowness (14 m.); Kendal (14 m.). Circular tours and afternoon and evening coach excursions are run to the Lake District and to the Morecambe entertainments.

Golf.—*Grange Golf Club*, Meathop Road and *Grange Fell Golf Club*, High Fell (*see* p. 18). Putting greens adjoining Promenade and at Berners Close.

Hotels.—*Grand; Grange; Crown; Netherwood; Graythwaite Manor; Commodore*
Places of Worship.—*St. Paul's Church, Roman Catholic, Congregational* and *Methodist Chapels.*

Tennis.—Public courts adjoining Promenade and at Berners Close. North Lonsdale Lawn Tennis Club.

This charming watering-place numbers a residential population of nearly four thousand. The promenade, nearly a mile and a half long, is well provided with seats and shelters, and at the western end are a bathing pool and tennis courts and bowling and putting greens. Had Nature endowed it with firm golden sands, Grange would have been an ideal resort for young children.

Grange has a higher temperature in spring than any other place in the North of England. Beautifully situated on the lower slopes of **Yewbarrow,** it is sheltered on the north and west by hills, and has a fine outlook over Morecambe Bay. The best view of the country is from the *Hospice* at the summit of **Hampsfell.** On the panelled walls within the hospice are inscribed verses descriptive of the scenery and the object of the building.

A mile south of Grange is **Kent's Bank** (*Kent's Bank Hotel*) which in olden times was the first *terra firma* landing-stage of the perilous low-water route over the sands from the south-east side of Morecambe Bay. What remains of the Abbot's Hall carries the mind back to pre-Reformation times, when the monks of Cartmel enjoyed the privilege of appointing the guide who conducted travellers thither. The building is supposed to have been erected for the special accommodation of the Abbot of Furness when he thus journeyed. At the Dissolution the revenues derived from this source were paid into the exchequer of the Duchy of Lancaster, and an official guide, styled in a charter of George III, "keeper, conductor, and governor over the sands," was appointed.

The huge, unwieldy form of **Humphrey Head,** four miles to the south from Grange-over-Sands, commands fine views. At its base is a mineral spring called Holywell. In a cave near by, known as Kirkhead, many implements of bone, stone, and bronze, and other prehistoric relics, have been found.

Cartmel

Two miles west of Grange, is said to have obtained its name (*Caermoel*, literally, "a camp among the hills") from an ancient British camp. Ecfreth, King of Northumbria, granted the whole region of Cartmel to St. Cuthbert, *with the Britons in it*. (Hotels: *King's Arms; Cavendish Arms; Royal Oak; Priory* (Guest).) Cartmel is a quiet old place, a cathedral city in miniature, happy in the possession of a fine old **Priory Church,** one of the few which escaped complete destruction at the Dissolution. The upper tower is remarkable, its angles facing the cardinal points of the compass.

The church possesses many points of architectural beauty, including a fine oak screen and choir stalls in excellent preservation. The carvings of the *misereres* are remarkable. There is a valuable library of ancient black-letter volumes in the vestry. The beautiful east window is believed to have been inserted in the reign of Henry VI.

Cartmel Priory was founded in 1188 by William Marshall, Earl of Pembroke, who expelled the French invaders after the death of King John. The monks are said to have been guided in their choice of the site by a supernatural voice which bade them erect the church "in a valley between two rivers, where the one runs north and the other south." The buildings and grounds once covered an area of 22 acres. Apart from the church, the gateway (date about 1330) and part of the wall only remain; this has been restored and is now open to the public (National Trust. *Small fee*).

The promontory on which Cartmel and Grange are situated is washed on the west by the combined waters of the Crake and the Leven, which drain the lakes of Coniston and Windermere. In the middle of the estuary is **Chapel Island,** with the remains of a chapel said to have been built by the priors of Conishead for the use of persons crossing the sands.

Ulverston

Banks.—*District; Midland; Barclays.*
Early Closing.—Wednesday.
Fairs.—Hiring fairs are held on the Thursday of Whitsun week and the Thursday on or after November 11th.
Golf Links.—Eighteen-hole course in Bardsea Park (2½ miles).
Hotels.—*Sun; King's Arms; Bay Horse, Railway; Lonsdale House.*

Market Day.—Thursday.

Places of Worship.—*St. Mary's, Holy Trinity, St. Jude's, Roman Catholic, Baptist, Methodist, Friends, Church of Christ,* and others.

A cinema, public hall, and facilities for most sports.

Ulverston (population 10,850) is situated on the northern shore of Morecambe Bay and on the southern side of the Lake District. It is the administrative centre and market town for the Furness District and is admirably situated as a centre for holiday making. Excellent road services radiate from the town to all parts of the Lake District and within easy reach lie Windermere, Coniston and Esthwaite Waters, the Coniston Mountains, the Duddon Valley and a host of charming villages. The town itself is close to the sea and surrounded by beautiful countryside. Facilities are available for bathing, boating, fishing and rock climbing. In Lightburn Park are tennis, bowling and putting facilities and an excellent 18-hole golf course is available just outside the town. Annual events of tourist interest include agricultural shows, sports and athletic events, hiring fairs, steeplechasing and hound trails. Dances in the Coronation Hall.

The Parish Church was founded in 1111 but was mainly

re-built in 1866. There is a Norman doorway, a late Perpendicular Tower, several interesting monuments, and some fine glass.

Above the town stands **Hoad Hill** (435 ft.) on which is a monument to Sir John Barrow, who was born in Ulverston in 1764. In 1792 Sir John Barrow accompanied an embassy to China and on his return wrote an account of the visit, which brought him no little fame. He was appointed Secretary to the Admiralty and occupied this position for forty years. He wrote a standard work on the subject of the "Mutiny on the Bounty." The monument, erected in 1850, is a replica of Eddystone Lighthouse, one hundred feet in height, and commands a magnificent view of the surrounding countryside.

Two miles to the south of Ulverston is **Conishead Priory.** The history of the Priory goes back to the time of Henry II, when it was established by Gamel de Pennington, but the present grand mansion on the site of the Priory dates only from 1821. There are nearly two hundred acres of grounds bordering the western shore of Morecambe Bay.

Swarthmoor Hall, built in 1580 in the Elizabethan style was the residence of Judge Fell, and it was here that the famous Quaker George Fox made his residence. After the Judge's death, George Fox married his widow and continued to live at Swarthmoor Hall. His bequest enabled the present Meeting House to be built at Rakehead near Ulverston. His wife is buried in the Friends' Burial Ground at Sunbrick about three miles from Ulverston.

Aldingham is a small coastal parish five miles from Ulverston. The church is well worth a visit and stands apart and simple in its antiquity. It has a lepers' squint, and an ancient 12th-century Southern Arcade of massive pillars, each probably made from a single stone. Nearby is **Gleaston Castle** (two miles from Aldingham). The castle ruins will repay inspection.

The direct route from Ulverston to Furness Abbey (see pp. 75–8) and Barrow passes through **Dalton,** a picturesquely-situated small town, the birthplace of George Romney, the portrait painter, whose grave in the churchyard is marked by a plain stone inscribed "Pictor Celeberrimus." He died at Kendal on November 15, 1802. There is also a modern and very pleasant coast road from Ulverston to Barrow, avoiding Dalton.

Greenodd to Coniston and Broughton

From Greenodd, three miles from Ulverston, a good road runs northward to the foot of Coniston Water at Water Yeat and continues close to the western shore, *via* Torver into Coniston. The name **Greenodd** has a Scandinavian origin; the "odd" (*i.e.* ness) being visible just by the station. The village is situated at the entrance to the pretty valley of the river *Crake*.

Soon after leaving Greenodd the road passes through the hamlet of **Penny Bridge.** At **Spark Bridge** are some wood turnery works. At **Lowick Green** the direct road from Ulverston joins that from Broughton. We next reach **Lowick Bridge,** with Lowick Church and Hall in the immediate neighbourhood. About a mile beyond is **Blawith Church;** and in another mile we reach the foot of the lake at Lake Bank.

The lake and the village of Coniston are described elsewhere (p. 68). For Broughton direct (*see below*) take the road running westward from Lowick Green and proceed over Gawthwaite Moor and *via* the village of Grizebeck.

The southern coast-line of the Lake District is penetrated by three estuaries—the Kent, the Leven and the Duddon. At the head of the Duddon estuary is—

Broughton-in-Furness

with a railway station on the main line at Foxfield, one mile distant. It is a small market town (*High Cross Inn; Old King's Head, Manor Hotel*) pleasantly situated on a slight eminence, three-quarters of a mile east of the Duddon. In the centre of the Market Square stands a stone obelisk to the memory of one John Gilpin, the donor of the site on which the square is built. The Church, dedicated to St. Mary Magdalene, is in the Early English style, and occupies the site of an old and interesting structure, removed in 1873. There is, however, still a fine Norman doorway on the south side.

Broughton Tower is a mansion standing on the site of the old castle of the Broughtons, a family who settled here in Anglo-Saxon days, and flourished under Normans and Plantagenets. A tower of the old castle and a portion of its dungeons yet remain, but the greater part of the house was rebuilt about 1750 or later. It is now in use as a special school for delicate children. There are several public footpaths through the park.

From Broughton several pleasing excursions may be made.

Ascent of Black Combe. This mountain is about five miles to the west. The road runs for the first mile north-west to Duddon Bridge, and then turns south-westward, passing through the hamlet of **Broadgate.** The walkers may proceed directly from Duddon Bridge to **Swinside** (where is a very fine pre-historic circle) by following a steep but pleasant path over the heathery fell and crossing two unbridged becks. Ascending the ridge in a south-westerly direction, and leaving **White Combe** (1,361 ft.) on the left, we make directly for the summit of **Black Combe** (1,969 ft.) from which there are extensive views. Descending the southern slope, we cross the high road from Broughton to Bootle, and reach the station at **Silecroft,** whence the return to Broughton can be made by rail and bus. (At Silecroft there are very fine sands at low tide.)

Broughton is also a favourite starting-point for the **Duddon Valley,** described under the Coniston excursions on p. 71.

Seven miles west of Broughton in a straight line, but farther by rail or road owing to the necessity of rounding Black Combe, is **Bootle,** a very different Bootle from that overlooking the Mersey, though its market charter dates from 1347. At Seaton Nunnery, a mile to the north, are the ruins of an early thirteenth-century Benedictine house. The whole area to the north is rich in relics of the past: ancient garths (enclosures), stone circles, beacons, cairns, etc.

Ravenglass

(*Pennington Arms*), is a small village, some eight miles north of Bootle, at the confluence here of the rivers Esk, Mite, and Irt. Pearl mussels used to be found here, and the fishing in these rivers is still good. The old custom of "riding the fair" was formerly observed on June 8. Across the estuary is a notable *Tern and Gull Sanctuary*, a local Nature Reserve, which may be visited by special permission from the Cumberland County Council, Carlisle.

The narrow-gauge **Eskdale Railway,** between Ravenglass and Dalegarth, near Boot, is a convenient means of access to Eskdale and also provides one of the "sights" of this part of Lakeland. There are intermediate stations at Muncaster, Irton Road, Eskdale Green and Beckfoot. Services are run during summer months.

Walls, the ruins of a Roman bath-house, about eight minutes' walk from the village, has attracted much attention from antiquaries. It was part of a large Roman camp, overlooking their western port at the end of the Roman road from Kendal, Ambleside and Hardknott.

On the southern slope of Muncaster Fell is **Muncaster Castle,** the seat of Sir William Pennington-Ramsden, Bt. It has been the home of the Pennington family since the middle of the thirteenth century. (*Grounds open daily Easter–June 30; July–August, Suns., Weds., Thurs. 1–6, Cnstle open Easter–August, Suns., Weds., Thurs., 2–5. Closed end of August. Admission 15p. Children 7½ p.)*

Just beyond the bridge crossing the line of the old packhorse road can be seen the stone monument marking the spot where a shepherd found King Henry VI wandering on Muncaster Fell after his defeat at the battle of Towton in 1461 and took him to Sir John Pennington's Tower, now the south-west tower of the present castle. The King gave Sir John an enamelled glass bowl for thus giving him shelter after he had been refused at Irton Hall; this glass bowl, known as the "Luck of Muncaster" is among the treasures of the Castle. Muncaster Church, of considerable antiquity, adjoins the park.

Waberthwaite Church is interesting as having been for centuries the chapel for Muncaster Castle, the wath or ford to that place being passable at low tide. The building has escaped restoration. In the churchyard is a pre-Norman cross-shaft with an interesting story.

The coastline continues northward over the estuary of the Esk to **Drigg.** The neighbourhood was formerly noted for its oaks, hence the name *derigh,* or *dergh* (Celtic, "oak").

The best road from Drigg to Wastwater follows approximately the course of the *Irt,* by Holmrook (where the river must be crossed) and **Irton,** the church of which is a conspicuous object for miles and in the churchyard of which an Anglian cross is still standing. The road to Wastwater leads straight forward past Irton Hall, over **Santon Bridge** and by the north-west foot of Irton Fell, and so past **Strands** (*see* p. 117).

Four miles beyond Drigg, on the coast-line, is—

Seascale

(*Scawfell, Wansfell, Inzievar*) a popular and attractive seaside holiday place. and golfing resort on the Cumberland coast There are good sands, and behind them a considerable grassy stretch, and the railway is less prominent here than in some other resorts. Accommodation is good, the sea-bathing and the golf quite the best near the Lakes. The 18-hole course extends for more than three miles along the shore. Eskdale, Ennerdale, Wastwater and Calder Abbey can be comfortably explored, the roads being generally excellent for cycling.

Two miles from Seascale is **Gosforth**, quite a considerable village with a notable ancient cross, dating about the year A.D. 1000, in the churchyard. Its sides are covered with curious figures and devices, showing a quaint admixture of the Norse and Christian religions.

Two and a half miles north-west of Gosforth is the village of—

Calder Bridge

on the *Calder*, a river which has its source in Copeland Forest to the east, and reaches the sea at Sellafield, about two miles to the west. Calder Bridge (*Sella Park; Stanley Arms*) is on the main road to Whitehaven, from which town it is scarcely a dozen miles south. Sella Park, between this village and the sea, was built by monks of Calder Abbey and is now an hotel. A short distance from the hotel a new road leads past the Winscale Plutonium Factory, and vast atomic piles where plutonium is made, and on to *Calder Hall*, Britain's first nuclear power station.

The ruins of **Calder Abbey** (Summer Sats.,Suns., 2-6) stand nearly a mile upstream from Calder Bridge. The remains, embowered in woods, consist of a Norman doorway, a central tower supported by pointed arches, and the walls of the south transept and the cloisters. The abbey was founded in 1134, under the auspices of the second Ranulph de Meschines, by a colony of monks from Furness Abbey, who about five years afterwards experienced a visitation from an army of Scots, and, having lost their all, returned to their mother abbey. Here they met with reproaches instead of succour. They therefore made their way to York and laid their case before the archbishop, who secured for them a patron in the person of a nobleman through whose instrumentality they were enabled to build Byland Abbey in 1142. Calder Abbey was afterwards occupied by a second colony from Furness who rebuilt the Abbey about 1220.

From Calder Bridge a road runs over Cold Fell due north for seven miles to **Ennerdale Bridge,** rather more than a mile west of **Ennerdale Water** (*see* p. 120).

St. Bees

(*Queen's, Abbot's Court, Albert, Sea Cote*) is a good excursion centre from which Ennerdale can easily be reached. There is bathing from the beach, golf, and sea fishing from the rocks below the Head. The name is taken from a monastery erected by St. Bega, an Irish recluse, in 650. The abbey church is still in good repair, having been spared, like Cartmel, at the time of the Dissolution, and restored in 1611 as the parish church. St. Bees was once renowned for its Theological College, established by Bishop Law in 1816, but now closed. Its *Public School* was founded by Archbishop Grindal in 1587.

St. Bees Head, the most prominent cape between Mersey and Solway, rises sheer out of the water to a height of more than three hundred feet. It forms the southern head of the bay of **Whitehaven,** among the safest harbours on the coast, from which steamers sail regularly to Belfast, the Isle of Man, Liverpool, etc. Whitehaven itself is a busy industrial town.

Cockermouth

(*Globe*, *Trout*, *Appletree*. Population 6,410. 18-hole golf-course.) Cockermouth, standing at the junction of the *Cocker* and the *Derwent*, has an abiding interest as the birthplace of Wordsworth. The house in which he was born (1770) stands on the north, towards the west end of the main street. It was in danger of being pulled down in 1938 and was saved by public subscription and vested in the National Trust. The house is open to visitors at Easter and on Mons., Weds. and Sats., from Whitsuntide–September 30 10.30–12.30 and 2–4.

The **Castle,** situated at the junction of the two rivers, was originally built soon after the Conquest, and additions have been made from time to time throughout the centuries. Part of the Castle is occupied by Lord Egremont and by the Egremont Estate Company; other parts and the ruins are open to the public 9.30–6, Sats. 9.30 to noon and 2–4, and Suns. 2–4.

The main street of Cockermouth crosses the river by a stone bridge. The town is one of the oldest in Cumberland and has been recognised as the market town and administrative centre for the surrounding agricultural area since the grant of its Market Charter in the reign of Henry III. The place is well served by road services.

There is good fishing in both rivers, the *Cocker* and the *Derwent*, for trout and salmon.

The Inland Section

KENDAL

Banks.—*National Westminster; Barclays; Lloyds; Midland; Yorkshire; William Deacon's; and Trustee Savings.*
Golf.—18-hole course on The Heights. *See also* p. 18.
Hotels.—*County; Kendal; Rainbow; Woolpack; Roebuck; Black Swan; Golden Lion,* etc.

Places of Worship.—*Parish Church, St. George's, St. Thomas's* and *All Hallows'*—all with Sunday services at 10.30 and 6.30. Chapels of most denominations.
Population.—20,160.
Post Office.—Stricklandgate.

Most tourists, hurrying to Lakeland, entirely overlook Kendal. They make a mistake. The "auld grey town" well merits at least a halt by the way. It is, moreover, a capital centre for cyclists and motorists, and the facilities it offers for road excursions, both in the cheapness of the fares and the beauty of the drives, challenge, on terms at least equal, many better-known resorts. In this latter respect, indeed, Kendal enterprise has developed recently to a degree as remarkable as it is creditable.

There are golf and cricket clubs to which visitors are admitted at moderate subscriptions, and bowls, tennis, putting, and angling in plenty. In Allhallows Lane is a swimming bath, where galas are held.

A hundred yards from Kendal Station is **Castle Dairy,** a fourteenth-century house, with alterations made in 1564. It is a well-preserved specimen of Tudor domestic architecture. Admission, 2 p.m.—4 p.m., *5p.*

The ruins of **Kendal Castle** form a conspicuous feature in the middle of the valley. Built in circular form in the twelfth century, some of the masonry dates back to the thirteenth century; the Castle and surrounding land belong to the town and are open to the public. The Castle was possibly the birthplace of Katherine Parr, the last of

Henry VIII's wives. The last surviving relic of this lady, her Book of Devotions, can be seen in the Town Hall.

Abbot Hall, in lovely surroundings, is a fine example of Georgian architecture. It has been well restored and is now an art gallery with collections of eighteenth-century furniture and some good paintings. A Folk Museum occupies the stable block.

The **Serpentine** is a delightful pleasure ground of about 18 acres, while the Kendal Fell Lands, adjoining the Serpentine woods, and partly occupied by golf links, are open to the public, giving practically unrestricted access to Cunswick Scar and along the cliffs to Scout Scar.

The glory of Kendal is the **Parish Church,** dedicated to the Holy Trinity. It is a handsome structure, partly thirteenth century but much restored, and consists of nave, chancel, and five aisles, this last feature being very unusual. The tower, 80 feet high, has one of the best peals of bells in the north. In the Parr Chapel is the remnant of an Anglian cross, probably dating from the ninth century.

In the Town Hall are several portraits by Romney, who served his apprenticeship in, and died at, Kendal. On the Milnthorpe Road is **Romney House,** where the painter lived his latter years. There is also an interesting **Museum** nearly opposite the railway station. A sufficient number of old-time buildings remain to give the town a fascinating air of antiquity. In former days Kendal was famous for its woollen manufactures, and Falstaff's allusion in *King Henry IV* to the "three misbegotten knaves in Kendal green" will be recalled in this connection. It is claimed that Stourbridge Fair was established by Kendal merchants. An important industry today is the making of boots and shoes.

Kendal is the centre of the **Mary Wakefield Musical Festival** and the **Lake District Festival,** both held in alternate years.

The Neighbourhood of Kendal

There are many places of great interest and beauty in the immediate vicinity of Kendal. Perhaps the best view of the town and valley, taking in the grand sweep of Morecambe Bay to the south-west, the Upper Kent valley, and the eastern range of the Lake District mountains, is from the top of Benson Knot. Good views can also be had at various points of the uplands intervening between the Kendal and Sedbergh road (the way of approach to Benson Knot) and the fern-clad summit of **Helm,** to the rear of Oxenholme Junction, from which place it can be reached in an easy half-hour's walk.

Undoubtedly the finest view-point in the neighbourhood of Kendal, however, is **Scout Scar** (two miles west of the Town Hall), from which may be seen a magnificent panorama of the Lakeland giants, including the Old Man, Scafell Pike, Bowfell, Great Gable, Fairfield and Red Screes. There is a tradition that it was from the topmost ridge of Scout Scar that John Martin painted his well-known picture, "The Plains of Heaven."

From the summit of the east corner of Scout Scar can be seen the roofs of **Sizergh Castle,** one of the finest ancient pele towers in Westmorland, and up to a recent date rich in superb and almost unrivalled oak carving, though one of the rooms is now in the Victoria and Albert Museum at South Kensington. Sizergh can be reached from Scout Scar by way of Brigsteer Wood, a very charming walk; but the best view of the Castle is from the Kendal and Milnthorpe road. Sizergh (National Trust) has been in occupation by members of the Strickland family from the thirteenth century. (*Open Wednesdays,* 2–5.45, *April to Sept., charge. Gardens open also Tues. and Thurs.*)

Nearly opposite Sizergh, on the east bank of the Kent stands the modern castellated mansion of **Sedgwick.** Near the north-eastern entrance to Sizergh Park a road leads to **Hawes Bridge,** which spans the river Kent at one of the most picturesque spots in the whole course of its journey from Kentmere to Morecambe Bay. There is a grim murder legend connected with the bridge.

About two miles farther down the Kent is **Force Bridge,** close to which is a long reach known as **Force Falls,** where the river tumbles over and among great boulders.

MOTOR RUNS FROM KENDAL

Motor coaches run to most of the villages and country towns in the neighbourhood, as well as into the heart of the Lake District which is entered at Windermere (8 miles).

We propose to refer specially only to the following:

1. Longsleddale

This is the first of the grand and romantic valleys of Westmorland encountered on entering Lakeland *via* Kendal, and there are few superior to it, more particularly for some distance beyond Sad Ghyll. When Wordsworth wrote his *Guide* a century or so ago, he mentioned as one of the advantages of this valley that it was "thoroughly free from the intrusion of art." Manchester Corporation, in taking their water through the dale, from the tunnel which carries it below the mountains from Haweswater, have covered their tracks most commendably.

The Shap road is followed for the first three and a half miles and commands the whole sweep of the Kent valley, Morecambe Bay, the south-eastern and eastern ranges of the Lake Mountains. Longsleddale begins at Garnett Bridge (on the river Sprint) and the valley is well named, being both long and narrow. Longsleddale Church (eight miles from Kendal) is modern and of no special interest; though small, it would probably hold all the inhabitants. There is a very pretty bit of waterfall at Sad Ghyll, another higher up under Buckbarrow, and several fine cascades right below **Harter Fell.** Near Buckbarrow Crag there is a happy hunting-ground for botanists in search of rare plants. The mountain way to Haweswater is over **Gatescarth Pass,** past the right shoulder of Harter Fell (*see* p. 112). Returning from Longsleddale to Kendal the traveller may make an interesting divergence by Burneside Hall, now a farm house, a good example of a fortified Pele Tower.

2. Levens Hall

This picturesque partly-Elizabethan mansion, about five miles south of Kendal on the Milnthorpe (A6) road, is famous in historic annals, rich in oak carving and works by old masters, and possesses a "topiary" garden planted in 1692 which still retains its original design. The owner lives in the Hall, but it is opened to visitors: May to mid-September, Hall, Tuesdays, Wednesdays, Thursdays and Sundays, 2–5. Gardens daily. Charge. In the noble park (right of way through main avenue) are rows of stately and venerable beeches and oaks, long stretches of broad grass-clad avenues, and shady foot-paths; it is the home of many species of birds and a fine herd of fallow deer. The river Kent winds through the park under Levens Bridge, past the front of the hall, onward to the waters of Morecambe Bay.

KIRKBY LONSDALE

Hotels.—*Royal; Green Dragon; Sun; Fleece; Red Dragon; King's Arms.*
Golf.—9-hole course. **Markets.**—Tuesday (cattle), Thursday (general).

Though beyond the borders of the Lake District, this attractive market town provides a popular excursion from Kendal (thirteen miles distant), and is also familiar to those approaching the district by the Skipton-Ingleton road. The country around is attractively varied—mountain, fell, and valley, with lovely stretches of the river Lune above and below the town.

The old bridge over the *Lune* probably dates from the thirteenth century, and is as strong today as ever, though a wider bridge built alongside in 1932 relieves it of the weight of modern traffic.

The **Church** dates from the reign of Stephen and is notable for its three Norman diamond-patterned pillars and an interesting door at the west end. Immediately beyond, from the Brow, overlooking the *Lune*, is one of the fairest prospects in England. The view was painted by Turner, and made popular by Ruskin. The mansion on the river bank, a short distance to the north, is *Underley Hall*, now occupied by St. Michael's College. A fine view of the house can also be obtained from a public pathway running through the park.

A former owner of *Casterton* (Castleton), a mile and a half north of the market, appears in the pages of *Jane Eyre* as head and founder of "the Clergy Daughters' School at Lowood, near Ingleton." The school started at Cowan Bridge, on the Settle road (during which time Charlotte Brontë was a pupil), but afterwards moved to Casterton.

Middleton Hall, five miles up the valley to the north, is an interesting example of fifteenth-century domestic architecture, now a farmhouse.

SEDBERGH

Hotels.—*White Hart; Bull; Golden Lion.*

Sedbergh, ten miles east of Kendal, is situated on the road approaching the Lake District *via* Hawes and the *Moorcock Inn*. The little town is a curious example of the twisty alleys and cramped buildings typical of the ancient north. The **Grammar School,** founded under Henry VII, after many vicissitudes has been reorganised as one of our great public schools. George Fox preached beneath the yews in the churchyard and gained a considerable following here.

To the south-east is **Dent,** a daintily antique village and dale, and north-west is another old-world countryside, **Howgill.** Practically every farm in this area has its ancient curiosities. *George Fox's Pulpit*, from which he preached to large congregations, is about two miles south of Lowgill Junction, on Firbank Fell.

There is golf at Sedbergh (*see* p. 18), and good fishing can

sometimes be arranged for, particularly in the moorland becks. A good deal of easy hill-walking can be enjoyed, the chief hills being the **Calf** (2,220 ft.), **Whernside** (2,419 ft.), and **Baugh Fell** (2,216 ft.). A certain amount of ski-ing is done from Sedbergh. The district lies within the Yorkshire Dales National Park. There are caravan sites available.

ORTON

Hotels.—*George* (licensed); *Waverley* (unl.).

Orton, about three miles north of Tebay, and six south-east of Shap, has been little spoilt by the "improvements" of the last generation and is built in the form of a rough square looking on to an island of pasture land and trees. Its streams and bridges are a pretty feature. It was a market town in the time of Edward I, and in its **Church** (All Saints) are medieval remains. The old **Hall** (now converted for residence) is much as it was in 1604, the date over the door. The present hall was built by Richard Burn, LL.D. (1709–1785), author of *The Justice of the Peace* and part author of Nicholson and Burn's monumental *History of Westmorland and Cumberland*, 1777. The district is rich in prehistoric remains.

SHAP AND DISTRICT

Shap

Hotels.—*Greyhound; King's Arms; Shap-Wells*, at Shap Wells.

Places of Worship.—*St. Michael's*; *Methodist Chapel.*

A feeling of disappointment will not improbably creep over the visitor on first arriving at this elevated village (872 ft.), though the air be pure, fresh, and bracing, and the surrounding hills grandly beautiful—a feeling that the place is bleak, bare and grey-looking, especially if the first visit is made on a sunless day. Shap is not one of those places which to look on is to love, but gradually the sense of disappointment wears away and, as a rule, a local saying, applied to natives, becomes a truism with regard to visitors, viz.: "Those who have tasted Shap bread and drunk Shap water will long to do so again." To the jaded man of business, or to the inhabitant of a town where the air is relaxing, the air of Shap serves as a capital tonic.

The old **Parish Church** has been much restored. So early as 1170 it was appropriated to Shap Abbey. The remains of a curious font with a shallow basin, dated 1757, and a sugar-loaf shaped cover of wood, are to be seen in the vestry. The low, embattled tower contains a sweet-toned peal of six bells. The registers date from 1559. An oak frame near the door bearing the initials P.L.W. (taken from one of the pews when the church was restored) is a reminder of a former Lord of the Manor, Philip, Lord Wharton, who fought against Charles I at Edge Hill, and died 1696. He was the father of the famous Whig statesman of William III's reign. Under Lord Wharton's will a number of Bibles and Prayer-books are annually distributed in Shap, the recipients being expected to have learnt the catechism and certain psalms.

Close to the Market Square is a quaint building on the west side of the main street, having half-moon windows with diamond-shaped panes. This, the Moot Hall, is the only picturesque building in the village. Originally a market cross stood on the site.

Shap was of old an important coaching centre, and several houses bear seventeenth-century dates, but, with one exception, little of historic or romantic interest attaches to them. The exception is the house known as **West Farm,** where Prince Charlie stayed a night in the rebellion of 1745. The landlady had certainly "taken in" the Prince in two senses, for in his household book was found the following entry:

> "17th Dec., at Shap, Tuesday. To ale, wine and other provisions, £4 17*s.* 0*d.*; the landlady, for the use of the house, £2. 2*s.*
> N.B.—The landlady a sad wife for imposing."

Altogether the Prince had not a very happy time in the Shap district, for when he and his army left Penrith they marched to Kendal in one day, and the Prince travelled the whole distance on foot (twenty-seven and a half miles). In crossing Shap Fells he was compelled to support himself by the shoulder belt of one of his stalwart Highlanders, an Ogilvie.

Shap Abbey

Open 9.30–4, 5.30, or 7. Sun. 2–4, 5.30, or 7, according to season. Admission free.

A mile from the village is Shap Abbey, the only abbey of which Westmorland can boast. To reach it leave the high road at the north end of the village, and keep on the Bampton road from which take second turning on left. Follow the lane for a short distance and the sight of the Abbey breaks in upon what has hitherto seemed a commonplace walk, save for the distant hills. At any time of the year the abbey tower, standing imposingly in the Lowther Valley, cannot fail to arouse admiration. The situation is highly suited for a retreat, for all is peaceful and undisturbed. The trees in the foreground, the Mardale hills beyond, and the river Lowther, near which the ruins stand, all give character to the scene. The ruins once in sight, follow the road leading over the bridge towards the abbey farm. The entrance to the abbey is opposite the tower. Car park.

The Abbey was founded about 1190 by Thomas, son of Gospatric, a member of a family having large possessions in Cumberland and Westmorland. A portion of these lands he gave to God and St. Mary Magdalene (to whom the Abbey is dedicated), and to the canons of the Præmonstratensian Order, for the purpose of building a house at Preston Patrick, in Kendal Ward. For some reason or other this monastery or abbey did not prove to Thomas's satisfaction, so, about 1200, he removed the "White Canons," as they were styled on account of their dress, to Shap, or Heppe, as it was then called. Sir W. H. St. John Hope, M.A., says (*Transactions of the Cumberland and Westmorland Archæological Society*)—

"The remains of the abbey consist almost entirely of the church and claustral buildings. The various offices that stood in the outer court have utterly perished, including even the gateway—a part of the buildings often spared. . . . The Church was begun very shortly after the foundation, that is *circa* 1200, and, as usual, at the east end. Probably an interval of seventy years elapsed between the commencement of the presbytery and the completion of the nave. . . . The west side, according to Buck's view, taken in 1739, had a large doorway, over which was a window of five lights with tracery in the head. Since then those features have been much altered; the tracery of the window has disappeared, and the jambs have been chopped down to the ground line, thus forming an arched opening to correspond with the tower arch. Above the window is a good canopied niche, with a hook in the back for the lost image (probably St. Mary Magdalene)."

The ruins are now in the guardianship of the Ministry of Public Building and Works.

The most notable of the later abbots was Richard Redman who was in turn Bishop of St. Asaph, Exeter and Ely, at the same time as Abbot of Shap, deputised for the head of the Præmonstratensian order in England and served as Privy Counsellor to Henry VII. The last abbot, Richard Baggot, or Evenwode, surrendered the Abbey on January 14, 1540, and secured a pension for himself and his convent.

The **Granite Works** and **Quarries** south of Shap are of considerable interest. The works are situated at the highest point of the London Midland Region's system, two miles from Shap. The quarries are at **Wasdale Crag** (the highest point of which is 1,749 ft. above sea-level), another two miles beyond the granite works. The beautiful felspathic granite from these quarries is in high repute for ornamental as well as for engineering and other purposes.

Reference is made in nearly every work on the district of Shap to **Carl Lofts.** Light may be thrown on the origin of the word "Lofts" by the following, culled from Sullivan's *Cumberland and Westmorland, Ancient and Modern:* The great boulders of the South of Ireland are accounted for . . . as "the giant's finger-stones." An old man of the neighbourhood once explained to an inquirer that the giants of old used to loft there—lofting being understood to mean throwing stones by heaving. There seems to be a connection between this explanation of the boulders and Carl Lofts (Carl's Lofts). Alas! Carl Lofts is now no more, though a few of the stones may be seen behind the old railway station and outliers elsewhere.

There is also a Druids' Circle half-way between Shap and the Toll Bar near the railway.

People unacquainted with the locality are apt to conclude that Shap and **Shap Wells** (*hotel*) are one and the same place. Shap Wells, however, is four miles south of Shap, and is not even in the parish of Shap.

EXCURSIONS FROM SHAP

1. To Gunnerkeld

To reach the Druids' Circle at Gunnerkeld, proceed along the Penrith road, over the Skew Bridge, until the first turning to the right, when a guide-post directs to Sleagill. Turn in the Sleagill direction, avoid the first turn to the left, and keep straight on until there comes into view a very rocky bit of country. Go through the gate on the left side of the road and follow a foot-path which leads through four fields. The Druidical remains are in the fourth field, at Gunnerkeld Bottoms. There are two circles, the inner very decidedly, the outer less well, marked.

2. To Bampton

Hotel.—*Crown & Mitre.*
Places of Worship.—*St. Patrick's Church, Methodist.*
Postal.—The post-town for the district is Penrith. Letters should be addressed Bampton, Penrith. There is a telegraph office in the village.

Bampton, close to the river *Lowther*, is a quiet village, about four miles from Shap by road and two and a half from Haweswater. There is a pleasant walk from Shap through the fields *via* Rosgill and Hegdale. Owing to its proximity to fishing streams and the lake, Bampton is a favourite resort of anglers. The **Church**, restored eighty years ago, was built in 1726. In the graveyard are some interesting records of famous Bamptonians; one especially notable, in the porch, commemorates the Rev. John Bowstead, fifty-six years master of the old Grammar School; a man who boasted, "I've eddecated three hundert priests, I hev, et hev eh"; and the old man certainly did turn out some first-rate scholars.

3. To Swindale and Mardale

Swindale, about three and a half miles west of Shap, over the fell (six miles by road), is well worth a visit. It resembles Mardale, save that it has no lake. At the head of the valley is a waterfall.

From Shap Abbey the route leaves the stream, passes through a gate 200 yards from the ruin and then crosses a common, over which there is no regular track. Take a south-westerly direction, keeping a clump of trees, at first prominent but shortly disappearing, well to the right. In about ten minutes the new Haweswater road is crossed and in another ten minutes the cart-track from Keld to Swindale is entered a little to the left of Tailbert farmhouse. Do not pass by the farmhouse but, where the track forks, keep to the greener left-hand branch, which gradually ascends the fellside and then, bending slightly to the left, descends obliquely into **Swindale.**

On the other side of the bridge the regular road up the valley from Rosgill is joined. Follow this for about three-quarters of a mile, and then turn up a horse track to the right, close to a ruinous farmhouse. This track climbs the steep part of the fell and when it has reached the level ground at the top becomes difficult to trace for a time. The best direction is to keep straight on in a line with the track by which you descended into Swindale, at the same time making for the most depressed part of the range you are crossing. The head of Haweswater then soon comes into view.

Mardale Church, a small and ancient building, in which the last service was held on August 18, 1935, was demolished in 1936 in preparation for the flooding of the site when Haweswater became a reservoir for Manchester. It was originally a daughter chapel under Shap Church and for many years the dead were carried to Shap for burial; consequently the route through Swindale which we have just described was always called the "corpse road."

HAWESWATER

Road Routes.—From Keswick, Patterdale, etc., the best route is *via* Penrith and the main trunk road (A6) towards Shap. At Lowther, however, turn off through the grounds of Lowther Castle to Askham and so to Haweswater by Bampton.

From Windermere and the South follow the Kendal-Carlisle highway (A6) as far as Shap, where turn off on left. Or continue along A6 as far as Lowther and thence as above.

Walking Routes.—From Windermere the way lies up Kentmere and over the Nan Bield Pass; from Ullswater the High Street range has to be crossed either by Fusedale and Weather Hill from Howtown; by Boardale Hause, Angle Tarn, and Kidsty Pike from Patterdale; or by Hartsop and Hayes Water over High Street. The best approach is from Shap.

Hotel.—*Haweswater.*

The Corporation of Manchester, in converting this lake into an artificial reservoir, made some very drastic changes.

Raising the level involved submerging the site of Mardale Church (demolished 1936), the *Dun Bull* at Mardale Green, and all the farms and houses in the valley. A new road was made along the south-eastern side of the lake as far as Gatescarthfoot, and the *Haweswater Hotel* was built rather more than half-way along it. The old road along the north-western side is now under the water, and in substitution for it there is a ramblers' path higher up the slopes of the fell. The scenic character of Haweswater has necessarily been altered by the disappearance of the farms and fields at the lakeside. Walkers entering the valley should be warned that there is not even a single house on the north-western side of the lake, and only the hotel on the south-eastern side.

About half a mile short of the dam the approach road from Bampton reaches Burnbanks, a small village created by Manchester Corporation, crosses the river and proceeds through Naddle Forest, a piece of native woodland with Wallow Crag rising ruggedly from its midst. From the hotel onwards the views across the lake to the High Street fells, including Kidsty Pike, are increasingly good, and finally Harter Fell, straight ahead, presents a striking front. At Gatescarthfoot the road ends, close to the head of the lake, and beyond this point there are only mountain tracks.

The dam, the only hollow structure of its kind in the country, is 1,550 feet long and 120 feet high.

The ramblers' path starts at Burnbanks, strikes up the

fellside to the right of the dam, and then carries on, sometimes near the lake, sometimes well above it, to Measand (where there is a concrete bridge at some pretty waterfalls), Whelter (the second concrete bridge) and Riggindale (the third concrete bridge). After Riggindale the path leaves a larch plantation on the left and climbs over a low shoulder from which the head of the lake is presently seen. (Mardale Church used to stand not far from the northern tip of this plantation.) The walk by the path is easy and pleasant and takes about two hours; the road is a good deal shorter.

PENRITH

Banks.—*Barclays; National Westminster; Lloyds; Midland;* and *Carlisle and North Western Counties' Savings Bank.*
Early Closing.—Wednesday.
Excursions.—Penrith is a good centre for excursions by coach, boat or rail. During the season there is a through connection by coach and boat between Penrith and Patterdale, *via* Pooley Bridge, (*see* p.105).
Golf.—18-hole course on Beacon Hill. For other courses, *see* p. 18.
Hotels.—*George; Castle; Hussar; Station; Strickland; Glen Cottage; Carleton; Clifton Hill* and numerous others.
Places of Worship.—*St. Andrew, Christ Church, Roman Catholic, Congregational, Friends, Presbyterian, Methodists,* and others.
Sports.—Golf, tennis, cricket, football, rugby football, bowls, swimming, shooting, fishing, hunting, horse riding, pony trekking.

Penrith is *the* junction for Northern Lakeland, and many railway travellers and motorists on their way to or from Scotland break journey here in order to see something of Ullswater and its surroundings.

The town, one of the oldest in the North, figured prominently in the wars between Scots and English, and was several times sacked—notably in the reigns of Edward III and Richard III. The latter monarch is reported to have lived on one occasion at the castle, and on another at the Gloucester Arms Hotel (Dockray Hall), over the doorway of which are his arms. The town is overlooked by the ruins of the **Castle,** supposed to have been built by Bishop Strickland and partly by the Nevilles. During the contest with Charles I it passed into the hands of the Commonwealth. The castle was subsequently dismantled, and became the property of the Dukes of Portland, who sold it in 1783 to the Duke of Devonshire. It has now become public property, the gardens being laid out as a park. The **Parish Church,** rebuilt in 1722, has an older tower, the higher portion of which was built by Warwick the King-maker. The church contains some interesting stained

glass. In the churchyard is a singular monument, called the **Giant's Grave,** traditionally affirmed to have been intended to perpetuate the memory of a legendary giant, one Owen Caesarius. It consists of two stone pillars (obviously ancient cross-shafts), standing at the head and foot of a grave, with four other stones (hogbacks) at the sides. If the grave contains the remains of the giant, he must have well deserved the title, for the stones are fifteen feet apart. Still, his proportions cannot have been Falstaffian, as the trench is less than a yard wide. Near these stones is another, the **Giant's Thumb**, so called from two holes at the top, said to be the size of the giant's thumbs. The stones are covered with pre-Norman carvings.

At **Eden Hall,** now demolished, in the valley of the Eden, was long preserved the celebrated "luck," a curious cup which forms the subject of a poem by Uhland, translated by Longfellow. The "luck" is now in the Victoria & Albert Museum in London. It has the appearance of a Venetian vase or a sacramental chalice, and legends are busy with its origin, for it is not certainly known how it came to the family. The generally-accepted tale is that a servant surprised some fairies dancing at the well, and seized the drinking-cup which they were using. As he declined to restore it, the offended fairies left it with him with a warning that—

"If e'er that glass should break or fall,
Farewell the luck of Eden Hall."

A bridge over the river of the same name at the village of **Eamont** divides the counties of Westmorland and Cumberland. In this neighbourhood, in which are many Lowthers, Howards, and Musgraves, much fighting and many stirring incidents have taken place, as the old castles testify.

The ruins of **Brougham Castle** are about one and a half miles south-east of Penrith. The site of Brougham is the *Brocavum* of the Romans; the castle was held by the Veteriponts and De Cliffords. Wordsworth's *Song at the Feast of Brougham Castle*, upon the restoration of Lord Clifford, the shepherd, to the estates and honours of his ancestors, is part of the household lore of the family. The outer walls of the castle are in fair preservation, the massive Keep and Gatehouse being of particular interest, but the interior marks the progress of time since 1617, when James I was a guest for three days. *Open Ministry standard hours, small charge.* A descriptive pamphlet is on sale at the castle.

Brougham Hall (formerly the seat of Lord Brougham), about three-quarters of a mile from the ruins of the castle, has been almost completely demolished.

It is unfortunate that **Lowther Castle**, five miles south of Penrith, has also been demolished except for the front façade. It was certainly one of the stately homes of England, where Royalty, foreign monarchs and distinguished visitors were frequently entertained.

From a point on the Kendal road about four miles south of Penrith a public road leads through the Park past the fine old Lowther Church and ancient Askham Hall, to the pretty village of **Askham**, whence one may continue to Bampton or to Pooley Bridge.

There are some interesting archaeological remains in the neighbourhood of Penrith, especially some six miles north-east of the town, on the summit of an eminence near Little Salkeld, the important "Druidical" circle called **Long Meg and Her Daughters.** The "daughters," some of them ten feet high, form a circle 350 yards in circumference, of sixty-six stones. Long Meg herself, a square unhewn column of red freestone, eighteen feet high, stands seventeen paces from the southern side of the circle.

From the Beacon (966 ft.), north of the town and about a mile from the station, a very extensive view is obtained.

Penrith to Ullswater

Many regular visitors to the Lakes declare—not without cause—that the route *via* Penrith, Pooley Bridge and Ullswater to Patterdale is the most picturesque one by which to enter the district.

Of the two roads from Penrith to Ullswater, the more pleasant follows the west bank of the Eamont. Passing the mansion of **Dalemain,** and its park, we cross a stream called the *Dacre*, or *Dacer*, which name it bore as early as the time of the Venerable Bede. It is a tributary of the Eamont, rising in the moorlands above Matterdale, and flowing down by the ancient mansion of Hutton John and Dacre Castle.

The alternate route from Penrith is by Pooley Bridge and follows the course of De Vaux's page, when—

"He passed red Penrith's Table round,
For feats of chivalry renown'd;
Left Mayburgh's mound and stones of power,
By Druids raised in magic hour;
And traced the Eamont's winding way
Till Ulfo's Lake beneath him lay."

Leaving the town, and crossing the bridge over the Eamont, we see in a field to the left an ancient earthwork known as **King Arthur's Round Table.** The table is a circular area about twenty yards in diameter surrounded by a fosse and mount, with two opposite approaches.

Excavations in 1937 by Professor R. G. Collingwood proved that there had been large posts, arranged in concentric circles twenty-five feet apart, apparently to support a roof. The post holes were still recognisable. In the centre there had been a burial, and it was assumed that the place may have been a Bronze Age crematorium.

On the opposite side of the road, and higher up the river, is **Mayburgh,** an area eighty yards in diameter, surrounded by a mound of pebbles. In the centre is a large block of unhewn stone, eleven feet high, believed to have been a place of Druidical judicature. The road continues through the pretty village of Tirril, leaves Barton Church on the right, and at Pooley Bridge crosses the river to the pier whence boats run up lovely Ullswater to Howtown and Patterdale. Barton is the ancient "mother" parish of all this area and the fine old church with its massive central tower is well worth a visit.

Regular bus services connect with the motor vessels on Ullswater, at Pooley Bridge.

Index

Where more than one reference is given, the first is the principal.

INDEX